D1044595

They Came to Bath

William Lowndes

REDCLIFFE

Bristol

First published in 1982 by
Redcliffe Press Ltd.,
49 Park Street, Bristol 1

Reprinted 1987

ISBN 0 905459 44 X

Printed in Great Britain by
Penwell Ltd., Callington, Cornwall.

Contents

I would like to acknowledge, gratefully, the help given to me by the staff of the Bath Reference Library, and by Mr. Sam Hunt, Curator of the Bath Museums Service.

Credits

All illustrations except those of Ralph Allen and Christopher Anstey (Victoria Art Gallery, Bath) are reproduced by courtesy of the National Portrait Gallery, London.
Cover illustration: Beau Nash — oil portrait by William Hoare *(courtesy:* Bath Museums Service, Bath City Council; *photo:* Sam Hunt).

For Joan

FOREWORD

One of the pleasures of Bath is to walk round its streets and to identify the houses lived in by celebrated residents or visitors. Nearly a hundred years ago Thomas Sturge Cotterell, an alderman and a former mayor of the city, conceived the idea of placing bronze tablets on houses occupied by famous people. His plan was adopted by the council and, in 1898, a grant of £250 was approved to erect forty-five tablets. The tablets were designed by Samuel Reay, a Bath architect, and their cost was rather less than £5 each—and that included the labour charges for fixing them in position on house walls. The first tablet was unveiled in 1898, and commemorated Sir William Herschel, astronomer-extraordinary, who lived and worked at No. 19 New King Street. Since then, something like seventy tablets have been placed on houses throughout the city, and they have provided a source of interest and enjoyment for many thousands of people.

One hopes that this book will increase that interest and enjoyment. It contains more than a hundred profiles of Bath's celebrities, most related to a number on the map, so that the positions of houses may be identified. An asterisk indicates the presence of a bronze tablet on a house; but almost half the profiles are of people who have not been so commemorated—although their contribution to the city's rich heritage has been considerable.

Many of the tablets have been darkened by the effects of weather and pollution, and it is often difficult to decipher their inscriptions. If this little book helps to avoid the need to peer at them at close range, it should be additionally useful.

Of the 125 people featured in this book, I have written at greater length about a dozen or so in *The Royal Crescent in Bath*.

ALLEN, Ralph (1693-1764)
Lilliput Alley (between North Parade Passage and York Street); *Prior Park*

Of the three men generally held to have been responsible for the city of Bath's sensational eighteenth-century development—Ralph Allen, Beau Nash and John Wood the Elder—Allen is arguably the most remarkable. He came to the city in 1710 from Cornwall, as assistant to the postmistress: and after succeeding her two years later, he became the youngest post-master in the kingdom, at a salary of £25 per annum. He won the patronage of General Wade in 1715, when he disclosed details of a Jacobite plot in the south-west; and with the general's financial support, he was able to institute a system of 'cross posts' that completely revolutionised the inadequate postal system, and made him a personal fortune.

In 1726 he bought the stone quarries at Combe Down, and built an ingenious railway to carry the huge blocks down to Bath, where the building renaissance, inspired by the genius of John Wood the Elder, was just beginning. This very astute enterprise earned him another fortune: and in 1735 he commissioned Wood to build Prior Park, a superb Palladian mansion overlooking the Widcombe valley and the city. The quarrelsome eccentric, Philip Thicknesse, described the house, perhaps with some justification, as 'a noble seat which sees all Bath, and which was built, probably, for all Bath to see'.

Allen was now a very wealthy man, and at Prior Park he entertained many of the famous poets, politicians, artists and men of letters of his time, including Pope, Gainsborough, David Garrick, Henry Fielding and the elder Pitt. Fielding, it is said, took him as the model for Squire Allworthy in *Tom Jones;* and Pope paid him a modest
8

compliment in the epilogue to his *Satires* with this couplet:

> 'Let humble Allen, with an awkward shame,
> Do good by stealth, and blush to find it fame'.

Whether by stealth or not, Allen was a warm-hearted philanthropist contributing generously to many worthy causes. He donated £1,000 towards the building of the Bath Hospital, as well as the stone from his quarries; and Fielding described him as 'a munificent patron, a warm and firm friend . . . hospitable to his neighbours, charitable to the poor, and benevolent to all mankind'.

What remains of his town house in Bath can still be seen, in Lilliput Alley, close to the Abbey. From the end of the alley, the narrow but splendid Palladian east front can just be glimpsed: and if the visitor turns round at this point he will see, on the slopes of Claverton Down, the folly that Allen built there. It is called Sham Castle, and is a façade with nothing behind it; its purpose was simply to enhance the romanticism of the view from his windows.

Ralph Allen was an outstanding businessman, and a legendary patron and benefactor. He was Mayor of the city only once—in 1742—but his influence on its development was profound. He died in 1764, aged seventy-one.

ANDRE, John, Major (1751-1780)
22 the Circus

John André was born and educated at Geneva, and came to Bath when he was nineteen, living for a time with his family at No. 22 the Circus. He joined the army and served in America; and after being involved in negotiations with the American traitor Benedict Arnold, who was planning the betrayal of West Point to the British, he was captured by the Americans and hanged as a spy. Strong pleas for mercy were made on his behalf, on the grounds that he was unaware of the extent of his complicity; but they all failed, and even his request to die by the bullet, like a soldier, was refused.

André, we are told, was handsome, chivalrous and highly intelligent, and his untimely death provoked a good deal of anger and resentment in England. In America, too, there were many who believed that his involvement in the plot was minimal, and that he should not have been condemned to death. A monument to his memory was later erected in Westminster Abbey.

ANNE, Queen (1665-1714)
Abbey Church House (demolished 1755)

During the last three hundred years there have been several royal visits to Bath. Queen Elizabeth I came in 1574, on one of her progresses through the western counties. In 1688 Princess Anne, later to become Queen Anne, visited the city, and returned with her husband, Prince George of Denmark, in 1692; they lodged at the old Abbey Church House, which stood just to the south of the Abbey, and was demolished in 1755.

Anne was seriously affected by gout throughout her life, and at her coronation in 1702, she had to be carried to Westminster Abbey by Yeomen of the Guard. Later that same year she came again to Bath with her husband, hoping to gain some relief from a course of the waters. The royal party was met outside the city by a mobile guard of honour, consisting of grenadiers and 'two hundred virgins, richly attired like Amazons with bows and arrows' and 'all of them

with a set of dancers who danced by the side of her
Majesty's coach, and waited upon her Majesty to the West
Gate of the city, where they were received by the Mayor and
corporation in their formalities'. On that occasion Queen
Anne performed the ceremony of 'touching for the King's
Evil'; thirty poor people suffering from scrofula were
touched on the neck by the Queen, in the belief that a cure
would follow. She was the last English monarch to perform
this ceremony. Macaulay, writing about the custom many
years later, remarked that 'there is nothing more credulous
than misery'.

Her gout, unfortunately, was not assuaged. But there can
be no doubt that her patronage of Bath in 1702 and 1703
was chiefly responsible for the remarkable increase in the
number of fashionable visitors to the city during the years
that followed.

ANSTEY, Christopher (1724-1805)
*5 Royal Crescent

In 1766 a small book, *The New Bath Guide,* was published
by Dodsley, a London bookseller. It was written by a
country squire from Cambridgeshire called Christopher
Anstey, and it became an immediate best-seller. The book
was not a guide in the accepted sense of the word; it was a
satirical review, in verse, of fashionable society in Bath in
the mid-eighteenth century, and its broad humour found a
receptive audience in London and Bath, where it was widely
read and discussed. Ten editions appeared during the
decade following its publication, and Anstey achieved a
modest measure of fame.

He was born at Brinkley in Cambridgeshire in 1724, and
was educated at Eton and King's College, Cambridge,

before settling down to manage his father's estates. The idea of the book was conceived after a visit to Bath to take the waters; and following its remarkable success, he came with his wife and children to live permanently in the city, taking one of the new houses that had just been erected by John Wood the Younger in Royal Crescent. The bronze tablet on No. 5 states that this was the house he occupied; but the city's early rate books seem to indicate that No. 4 was his house—although for some reason he paid the rates of No. 5 until 1789. In 1792 he moved to a house in the recently completed Marlborough Buildings, and there he lived until the year of his death in 1805.

His marriage was a successful one, and he and his wife lived contentedly together for nearly half a century; he described her as 'the pattern of virtue, and the source of all my happiness'. There were thirteen children of the marriage, but only eight survived their father.

A portrait of Anstey hangs in the magnificent Banqueting Room in the Guildhall at Bath. It was painted by William Hoare, and it shows a dark-haired, good-looking man in early middle age; he wears a sage-green coat, braided with gold, and a long white waistcoat, unbuttoned at the top, into which his left hand is thrust, in the Napoleonic manner. His unlined, fresh-complexioned face has an undeniable air of tranquility and contentment. He looks every inch a successful and happy man—a best-selling author, savouring the acclaim his work had brought him.

Oddly enough, he wrote nothing else of consequence after *The New Bath Guide.* The little book remains his memorial, and the justification for the tablet that is dedicated to him in Poet's Corner, in Westminster Abbey. It can still be read with much pleasure and amusement.

ARTHUR, Prince, Duke of Connaught (1850-1942)
Pulteney Hotel, Great Pulteney Street

The Duke of Connaught was the third son of Queen Victoria. He first came to Bath in 1881 with his wife, who was formerly Princess Louisa of Prussia, and the royal couple returned in 1909 to attend the Bath Historical Pageant. The Duke spent several weeks in the city in 1935 and 1936, when he came for the cure, and for the excellent orchestral concerts that were regularly given in the Pump Room at this time; on one occasion Sir Thomas Beecham conducted the orchestra of fifteen players in Borodin's *Polovtsian Dances.*

The Duke stayed at the Pulteney Hotel in Great Pulteney Street, formerly Stead's Hotel. The building has now been converted into luxury flats, and given the appropriate name of Connaught Mansions.

AUSTEN, Jane (1775-1817)
*4 Sydney Place

There are four houses in Bath that can claim to have accommodated Jane Austen during her active association with the city—an association that lasted approximately six years. In the summer of 1799 she stayed with her mother at No. 13, Queen Square for a month. A year later her father, the Rev. George Austen, gave up his living at Steventon in Hampshire, and decided to retire to Bath. A suitable house was found at No. 4, Sydney Place, and the family stayed there until the expiry of the lease three years later; a bronze tablet on the wall of the house identifies it as Miss Austen's principal domicile in the city. A short lease was then taken

13

on No. 27, Green Park Buildings, where Jane's father died in January, 1805; and afterwards Mrs. Austen and her daughters moved to No. 25, Gay Street. Little more than a year later, in the summer of 1806, they left Bath permanently, moving first to Clifton and Southampton, and finally, in 1809, to the little village of Chawton in Hampshire, where Jane spent eight happy and productive years before her death in 1817.

She never liked Bath. Some time after leaving the city, she wrote to her sister Cassandra: 'It will be two years tomorrow since we left Bath for Clifton, with what happy feelings of escape!' And perhaps she was mirroring her own feelings when, in *Northanger Abbey,* she has Isabella Thorpe confiding to Catherine Morland: 'I get so immoderately sick of Bath; your brother and I were agreeing this morning that though it is vastly well to be here for a few weeks, we would not live here for millions'. Yet, in spite of her obvious dislike of the city, the major parts of two of her novels—*Northanger Abbey* and *Persuasion*—are set in Bath, and the life she herself led there is perfectly reflected in the pages of both of them.

BALLARD, Admiral Volant Vashon (1774-1829)
34 Park Street

Bath provided a haven for many retired admirals during the nineteenth century, and Ballard is by no means the most distinguished—although few of them could have claimed more unusual christian names. He fought with Lord Howe at the celebrated action against the French in 1794 which became known as the 'Glorious First of June', and was promoted rear-admiral in 1825. Later, he lived at No. 34 Park Street; and when he died in October 1829, the *Bath*

Chronicle announced the fact with casual brevity: 'Died at Exmouth, Admiral Ballard, of Park Street in this city, and Coates Hall, Yorkshire'.

BARKER, Benjamin (1776-1838)
*16 Bathwick Street

Benjamin Barker followed the career of a painter, although he was never as successful as his elder brother Thomas, who was known as 'Barker of Bath'. He lived for a time at No. 16 Bathwick Street (where there is a bronze tablet), and then built himself a house on Bathwick Hill; Queen Charlotte is said to have visited him there when she came to Bath. Eventually he moved to Totnes in Devon, and died there in 1838.

BARKER, Thomas (1769-1847)
*Doric House, Cavendish Road

'Barker of Bath', as he was called, was a successful artist who lived and worked in the city for most of his life. He never approached the eminence of Gainsborough or Lawrence but, as a nineteenth century critic remarked, 'if not a great painter, he certainly was an uncommonly good one'. William Beckford bought several of his paintings, and Peel awarded him a pension in 1846. His most celebrated work was *The Woodman;* but in 1969, when a small collection of his wash drawings came under the hammer at Sotheby's, they realised only £15.

He lived at Doric House, at the top of Cavendish Road, an

15

impressive dwelling that housed a gallery as well as his studio. In 1825 he painted a huge fresco, thirty feet long and twelve feet high, on the wall of his dining room, illustrating the massacre of the Sciotes by the Turks in 1822. Examples of his work can be seen in the Victoria Art Gallery and the Royal Crescent Hotel.

BECKFORD, William (1759-1844)
19 and 20 Lansdown Crescent

No record of English eccentrics would be complete without a chapter on William Beckford. He had a passion for building towers and creating enormous gardens; he was a recluse who, nevertheless, fathered natural children with an abandon that shocked even the eighteenth century; he bought Gibbon's library at Lausanne, and shut himself up for a year to read through it; and when he rode out at Bath, top-hatted and mounted on a splendid Arab horse, he was generally preceded by his steward and two grooms carrying long whips, with a further two grooms bringing up the rear.

All these extravagances, of course, needed money, and Beckford was a very rich man indeed. His father was a millionaire sugar planter who was twice Lord Mayor of London; and when he died, he left William £27,000 and the magnificent family estate at Fonthill Gifford in Wiltshire. Here Beckford built a gigantic 300-foot tower, enlarged the garden, and spent twenty years amassing a huge collection of *objets d'art;* in 1823 it was disposed of in a sale that lasted thirty-seven days, and prompted Hazlitt to describe its contents as 'a desert of magnificence, a glittering waste of laborious idleness'.

Beckford, however, was a shrewd collector and dilettante;

16

Ralph Allen—engraving from a painting by T. Hudson.

Christopher Anstey—portrait by William Hoare.

Jane Austen—portrait by Cassandra Austen.

William Beckford—portrait by Sir Joshua Reynolds.

he had an aptitude for grandiose landscape gardening, and he was an author of considerable merit. As a young man he wrote a novel called *Vathek;* it is an oriental fantasy, telling the story of a caliph who sold himself to the powers of evil, and it is still widely regarded as his masterpiece.

A serious decline in revenues from his Jamaican sugar plantations obliged him to sell Fonthill in 1822. He came to Bath when he was sixty-three, and took two houses in Lansdown Crescent to which, as a contemporary noted, 'was added a gallery thrown over an archway, constituting the prolongation of a magnificent library'. On Lansdown Hill, overlooking Bath, he built another tower, not as gigantic as Fonthill, but impressive enough; it still attracts admiring visitors. His tomb can be seen nearby.

BELMORE, Mary, Countess of (1755-1841)
17 Royal Crescent

Lady Belmore lived at No. 17 Royal Crescent for thirty years until her death in 1841 at the age of eighty-six. For a long time she presided over balls held in the Assembly Rooms; and it was here that Dickens must have encountered her, probably in 1835. He completed *Pickwick Papers* shortly afterwards, and immortalised the dowager countess as Lady Snuphanuph in the chapters of the novel that deal with Mr. Pickwick's experiences in Bath.

BERRY, Admiral Sir Edward (1768-1831)
2 Gay Street

On September 25th, 1797 Nelson, after losing an arm at Teneriffe, was received by George III, and invested with the

Order of the Bath. He was accompanied at the levée by one of his most trusted captains, Edward Berry; and when the King remarked that he had lost his right arm, Nelson replied 'But not my right hand, as I have the honour of presenting Captain Berry'—thus gracefully acknowledging his debt to an admired friend and colleague. Berry served for many years with the admiral, and distinguished himself on several occasions; he was Nelson's flag-captain at the battle of the Nile, served at the blockade of Malta in 1800, and commanded the *Agamemnon* at Trafalgar. After being created a baronet in 1806, he was later awarded the KCB, and promoted rear-admiral in 1821. On his retirement from the navy, he lived in Bath at No. 2 Gay Street, from 1828 until his death in 1831.

BROOKE, Sir James (1803-1868)
*1 Widcombe Crescent

The 'White Rajah of Sarawak', as he was known, was born at Benares in India, but spent much of his early life in Bath, at No. 1 Widcombe Crescent. After returning to the far east and serving in the Burma war, he sailed in a private schooner to Borneo in 1838, and proceeded to Sarawak, where he was courteously received by the authorities. Two years later he returned, and was invited to undertake the government of the country. The reforms he introduced improved conditions greatly, and although he was accused of cruelty and illegal conduct, his authority was never undermined. He revisited England in 1847, and was awarded the KCB, and appointed consul-general of Borneo and governor of Labuan. He severed his links with Sarawak in 1863, five years before his death.

A bronze tablet on the façade of No. 1 Widcombe Crescent commemorates his stay there.

BURDETT, Sir Francis (1770-1844)
16 Royal Crescent

Sir Francis Burdett lived at No. 16 Royal Crescent from 1814 until 1822. As a politician, he was an ardent champion of electoral reform at a time when it was crucially needed, and he worked tirelessly throughout his life to expose abuses of power wherever he encountered them. As a baronet whose favourite recreation was fox-hunting, he seems an unlikely standard-bearer for such nineteenth-century ideals as prison reform, freedom of speech, and the abolition of flogging in the army; but he served two terms of imprisonment for his outspoken views, and was heavily fined. He never lacked the courage and determination to challenge corruption in public affairs; in 1809, when the Duke of York was involved in the unsavoury business of bartered army commissions, he seconded the motion in the House of Commons for an enquiry into the Duke's behaviour. He was MP for Westminster then, and represented the constituency for thirty years. No politician of his day had greater integrity.

BURDETT-COUTTS, Angela Georgina, Baroness Burdett-Coutts (1814-1906)
16 Royal Crescent

The deep concern for social reform that motivated Sir Francis Burdett was inherited by his daughter, Angela

Georgina. She lived at No. 16 Royal Crescent for the first eight years of her life, and later as Baroness Burdett-Coutts, became celebrated for her great philanthropy. Hundreds of worthy causes benefited from her generosity. She administered several charities, endowed St Stephen's Westminster, and other London churches and, as a lifelong lover of animals, gave active support to the work of the RSPCA. At her instigation, sewing and cookery were introduced into the curricula of elementary schools: and she even helped the costermongers of Bethnal Green in East London by providing stables for their donkeys.

She was, of course, immensely wealthy; as a granddaughter of Thomas Coutts, the celebrated banker, she was known as 'the richest heiress in England'. Later, she added his name to her own, and in 1871 she was raised to the peerage in recognition of her invaluable work. She was an indefatigable hostess, and there were few outstanding figures of the day who did not share the hospitality of her table; she was intimate with the royal family, the Duke of Wellington , Sir Robert Peel, Disraeli, Gladstone, Dickens, Sir Henry Irving and many others. She died in 1906 at the age of ninety-two, and was buried in Westminster Abbey.

BURKE, Edmund (1729-1797)
*11 North Parade

The great eighteenth-century statesman and political philosopher often stayed at Bath, chiefly for reasons of health. In 1756 he underwent medical treatment by Dr Christopher Nugent, who offered him hospitality at his home, Circus House, at the corner of Bennett Street and the Circus. Here Burke met the doctor's daughter, Jane Mary Nugent, and married her the following year, 1757; their younger son, Christopher, was named after Dr Nugent.

Burke was elected MP for Bristol in 1774, and served the city in that capacity for six years. He was a powerful speaker; Dr Johnson said of his conversation: 'He does not talk from a desire of distinction, but because his mind is full'. He abhorred extremism in politics, and never approved of the French Revolution; until the end of his life he remained a hostile opponent of the French state, and his views in this context lost him the close friendship of Charles James Fox and Sheridan.

Early in 1797 his health declined seriously, and he came again to Bath, staying at No 11 North Parade. He had always vigorously supported the campaign against slavery, and shortly before he died Wilberforce, who was then in Bath, visited him frequently. In May 1797 he wrote to a friend: 'I have been in Bath these four months to no purpose and am, therefore to be removed to my own home at Beaconsfield tomorrow, to be nearer a habitation more permanent, humbly and fearfully hoping that my better part may find a better mansion.' He died two months later, in July 1797.

The bronze tablet on the wall of No 11 North Parade was unveiled in October 1908, by Mr Whitelaw Reid, the American ambassador.

BURNEY, Fanny (later Mme d'Arblay)
(1752-1840)
14 South Parade

Fanny Burney was a prolific writer from an early age until her death, and her letters and diaries afford fascinating glimpses of English society in the latter half of the eighteenth century and the early years of the nineteenth.

She loved Bath, and visited the city frequently. In 1780, two years after the publication of her first, and best-known novel, *Evelina*, she stayed at No 14 South Parade with Mr and Mrs Thrale, the great friends of Dr Johnson. A bronze tablet on the house commemorates this visit.

She married General Alexandre d'Arblay, a French emigré, when she was forty, and lived with him in France until he was seriously wounded, fighting against Napoleon in the Waterloo campaign. They then returned to England and settled in Bath until d'Arblay's death in 1818. Earlier, she had written to a friend: 'I wish to live in Bath, wish it devoutly, for at Bath we shall live, or nowhere in England. Bath is . . . the only place for us since here, all the year round, there is always the town at command and always the country for prospect, exercise and delight'. She died in the city she loved so well, at the age of eighty-seven, and was buried at Walcot Church.

CHARLOTTE, Queen (1744-1818)
*93 Sydney Place

George III's queen came to Bath to take a course of the waters in November, 1817, the year before her death. A house was taken for her at No 93 Sydney Place, and lavishly equipped; and a second house at No 103 Sydney Place was reserved for her entourage, and for the Duke of Clarence, who arrived in the city on the same day. Bath welcomed the royal party enthusiastically and a contemporary, after describing the decorations, noted that 'tho' the streets were crowded to an excess, not the least riot or confusion appeared; nor were groups of well-dressed females annoyed in their perambulations by the throwing of squibs or the firing of guns'.

But the discreet merriment was short-lived. A few days after her arrival the Queen was informed of the death, in childbirth, of her grand-daughter, Princess Charlotte, and the royal party left at once for Windsor. Queen Charlotte returned to Bath three weeks later, and stayed quietly at Sydney Place for nearly a month. She was seventy-three at this time, and in failing health. Her death occurred during the following year, 1818.

CHESTERFIELD, Philip Dormer Stanhope, 4th Earl of Chesterfield (1694—1773)
3A and 4 Pierrepont Street

Philip Dormer Stanhope, fourth Earl of Chesterfield, was a statesman and man of letters who visited Bath regularly for a period of thirty years, living at No. 3A and No. 4 Pierrepont Street. He came to the city primarily for health reasons; the waters, he hoped, would assuage his gout and dispel the vapours. But he enjoyed himself, too—gambling, strolling along the parades, and attending the balls at the old Assembly Rooms. On one of these latter occasions he witnessed a haughty couple, both members of the nobility, gravely dancing a minuet; and later he told a friend: 'They looked as if they were hired to do it, and were doubtful of being paid'.

For many years he wrote regularly to his natural son, Philip Stanhope, giving him paternal advice on manners, duty and deportment. The letters—several of them addressed from Bath—are written in an elegant, intimate style that perfectly reflects the social atmosphere of the eighteenth century; since they were collected and published, they have been widely recognised as Chesterfield's major literary work. Dr. Johnson, however, thought otherwise; they were, he said, disgraceful, and 'taught the morals of a whore, and the manners of a dancing master'. They can, nevertheless, still be read with a great deal of enjoyment.

CHUDLEIGH, Elizabeth, Duchess of Kingston (1720-1788)
5 South Parade

She was a beautiful bigamist, and a friend of William Pulteney, who afterwards became Earl of Bath. When she was twenty-four, she secretly married Lord Augustus Hervey, a lieutenant in the navy. They quarrelled and separated, and more than twenty years later she married Evelyn Pierrepoint, second Duke of Kingston; they lived for a time at No. 5 South Parade, and the Duke died there in 1773, leaving Elizabeth as heiress to his property. In the following year she was accused of bigamy by Kingston's nephew, and was tried by her peers in London; Westminster Hall was so crowded that the Yeomen of the Guard had to be reinforced by troops. She was found guilty; but the peers, we are told, were 'so moved by her penitence and beauty' that they ordered her only to pay costs. After the trial she lived abroad in Rome and other cities and visited Catherine the Great in Russia. She died in Paris in 1788.

CLARENCE, Duke of (1765-1827)
103 Sydney Place

When Queen Charlotte, consort of George III, visited Bath in 1817, she was accompanied by her third son William, Duke of Clarence, who lodged at No. 103 Sydney Place. The visit was a brief one, marred by the news of the death, in childbirth, of Princess Charlotte, the daughter of the Prince Regent. The royal party left for Windsor almost immediately.

Princess Charlotte's death had a special significance for the Duke of Clarence. Because almost all of George III's children were dead, and Charlotte was the only child of the Prince Regent, his prospects of eventually succeeding to the throne were considerably enhanced. He did, in fact, become William IV on the death of his brother, then George IV, in 1830. A bronze tablet on the façade of the house in Sydney Place commemorates his brief stay there.

CLIVE, Robert, Lord Clive (1725-1774)
14 the Circus

In 1744, when he was a youth of nineteen, Robert Clive arrived in India, as a penniless clerk in the service of the East India Company. Later he joined the army, and his courage and determination won him rapid promotion. Within ten years he was a lieutenant-colonel; and when he won the crucial battle of Plassey in 1757, he laid the firm foundations of British rule in India. He was MP for Shrewsbury from 1760 until his death, and was created Baron Clive in 1762.

From 1767 he was constantly in Bath and lived for some

time, 'in a little pomp', at Westgate Buildings. Then, in the year of his death, he took a house at No. 14 the Circus. He was broken down in health, as a result of his long service in India, and the mental strain he had undergone following bitter attacks on his record from politicians and others. His constitution had been seriously undermined by epileptic fits, and by his addiction to opium; and because of these constraints, he was unable to take the waters, for which he had specially come to Bath. In November 1774 he returned to London, and committed suicide at his house in Berkeley Square.

The bronze tablet on the Circus house was unveiled by Field-Marshal Lord Roberts in September, 1902, when he visited Bath to receive the Freedom of the city.

COBBE, Lady Betty (1735-1792)
22 Marlborough Buildings

Lady Betty Cobbe, who lived at No. 22 Marlborough Buildings, was well-known in Bath in the late eighteenth century, because she was said to have been involved in a most unusual ghost story. In fact, it was Lady Betty's grandmother, Lady Beresford, who encountered the ghost; Lady Betty, before her marriage, had inherited the title of Lady Beresford, and when Sir Walter Scott wrote a story about the incident, she was confused with her grandmother. She was frequently asked to describe the experience, and eventually found the whole business a source of annoyance.

Briefly, the story was this: the elder Lady Beresford awoke one night to find the ghost of an ancestor sitting at the foot of her bed. The apparition lectured her at some length on orthodox theology, and at one stage touched her
26

wrist to emphasise the point. The wrist shrivelled alarmingly, and never recovered; and Lady Beresford was obliged to wear a black ribbon round it for the rest of her life, to conceal the marks of the ghost's fingers.

Lady Betty, it seems, could have dispelled much of the confusion by leaving her wrists uncovered. But she never did, and she continued to be identified with the ghost's victim. She probably enjoyed the notoriety for a time, but there can be no doubt that it palled eventually. Later in her life she received a letter from a lady-in-waiting to Queen Charlotte, requesting full details of the story. She replied brusquely, saying that 'she presented her compliments, but was sure the Queen of England would not try to pry into the private affairs of her subjects, and she had no intention of gratifying the impertinent curiosity of a lady-in-waiting'.

DE QUINCEY, Thomas (1785-1859)
6 Green Park

De Quincey spent three years of his boyhood in Bath, where he lived with his widowed mother at No. 6 Green Park. For much of this time he attended the grammar school in Broad Street, but was obliged to leave when a prefect struck him on the head, and caused permanent damage that was to affect him throughout his life. He was sent to Manchester Grammar School in 1801, and eventually went up to Worcester College, Oxford, where he matriculated. His literary output thereafter was chiefly confined to magazines and journals; but he was now taking opium regularly, and in 1821 his masterpiece *Confessions of an English Opium Eater* was published. It made him famous; but he lived in an unworldly, unorthodox fashion, giving all his money to beggars, ignoring bills and letters (he usually changed lodgings rather than deal with them), and indulging his passion for opium and long nocturnal walks. He died peacefully at Edinburgh in 1859.

A bronze tablet on No. 6 Green Park, with the inscription 'Here lived Thomas de Quincey, 1796-1799' has been removed.

DICKENS, Charles (1812-1870)
35 St. James's Square

The man whose novels have probably been read by a greater number of people than any other English works of fiction, was no stranger to Bath. As a young parliamentary reporter, he visited the city in the spring of 1835, to report a speech by Lord John Russell for the *Morning Chronicle;* and on that occasion he stayed at the "Saracen's Head" in Broad Street. Later, he often visited his close friend, Walter Savage Landor, at 35 St. James's Square. He was there in 1840, and is said to have conceived the character of Little Nell in *The Old Curiosity Shop* during his stay. *Pickwick Papers* had already firmly established his fame as a novelist, and in one or two chapters of this celebrated novel the social life of Bath was brilliantly satirised, with Mr. Pickwick taking the waters, Sam Weller, his faithful servant, declaring them to have 'a wery strong flavour o' warm flat irons', and Mr. Dowler and Mr. Winkle getting involved in a hilarious chase round the Royal Crescent.

Later in his life Dickens grew to dislike Bath—for a reason that now seems remarkably superficial. He was present in the Assembly Rooms when Bulwer-Lytton's play *Not So Bad As We Seem,* was performed by the Guild of Literature.
28

Dickens was a member of the Guild, and had given advice on certain aspects of production; and when the play was coldly received by the audience, and awarded poor notices in the local press, he was deeply displeased. He never forgave Bath from that moment.

A bronze tablet commemorating his visit to Landor's house, adorns the façade of No. 35 St. James's Square. It was unveiled in 1903, on February 7th (the novelist's birthday), by a representative of the Dickens Fellowship.

DISRAELI, Benjamin, 1st Earl of Beaconsfield (1804-1881)
8 Brock Street

Disraeli visited Bath for the first time with Edward Bulwer-Lytton, later Lord Lytton, in January, 1833. They are said to have stayed at the "White Hart"; but a letter that Disraeli wrote from Bath at that time casts some doubt on this assumption. 'We have a lodging at £2 per week in an unfashionable part of the town' he wrote, 'with no servant and do everything but cook our own dinners, to which Bulwer was very inclined—we have two sitting-rooms, and scribble in solitude in the morning until two—I have written about fifty pages of a pretty tale about Iskander, which will be a fine contrast to Alroy'. This certainly does not seem to indicate the 'White Hart', which was then presided over by Moses Pickwick, and noted for its comfort and service. The two scribblers, it would seem, lodged at a less prestigious establishment.

Alroy, the novel on which Disraeli was engaged at that time, was an exotic fantasy that was to be glowingly praised by William Beckford, although it never sold well; the 'pretty

29

tale about Iskander', a story of love, war and patriotism, was included in the novel. And Bulwer-Lytton was probably writing *The Last Days of Pompeii*, which was published during the following year, 1834.

In 1861, Disraeli bought a house in Bath, at No. 8 Brock Street. By that time he was a politician of considerable eminence; he had been Chancellor of the Exchequer and Leader of the House of Commons in Lord Derby's government two years previously, and he was soon to become Prime Minister. There would have been few opportunities, it seems, to visit Bath—although he must have intended to do so.

DU BARRÉ, Jean Baptiste, Vicomte (1749-1778)
8 Royal Crescent

In the churchyard at Bathampton, on the outskirts of Bath, there is a tombstone with an inscription that reads: 'Here rest the remains of Jean Baptiste du Barré. Obiit 18th November, 1778'. The brief statement is a sad little postscript to a heated quarrel that took place at No. 8 Royal Crescent, and ended tragically on Claverton Down, in the cold light of a November dawn.

The Vicomte du Barré came to Bath in the summer of 1778 with his wife and sister, and a Captain Rice, an Irish Jacobite whose grandfather had served in the French army. They took a lease on No. 8 Royal Crescent, and arranged lavish card parties in the house, hoping to profit from the gambling mania that gripped the city at that time. But one night they quarrelled over the sharing of £600 that they had won from a Colonel Champion, who lived at No. 29 Royal Crescent. Rice threw down his glove, the challenge was accepted, and both men hastily appointed seconds and made their way to Claverton Down, where pistols were primed. Du Barré fired first, and wounded his friend in the thigh. Rice's aim was more deadly; the Frenchman was hit in the chest, and died a few moments later.

Rice was subsequently tried at Taunton, but was acquitted and went to Spain. For the Vicomte, there was only a cold resting place in the churchyard at Bathampton.

FALCONER, Dr. William (1744-1824)
29 the Circus

In 1770 the physician to Chester Infirmary came to Bath, and took up residence at No. 29 the Circus; he was Dr. William Falconer, and he practised there for more than fifty years, as well as serving as physician to the Bath General Hospital from 1784 until 1819. He wrote essays on the efficacy of the Bath waters and, with Joseph Priestley, was co-discoverer of carbonic acid gas. One of his lesser claims to fame was to originate the lay-out for the planting of the five plane trees that dominate the Circus; before that time the area, now grassed, was covered with paving stones.

Falconer also established a small medical dynasty in Bath. His son, Thomas, qualified as a doctor, and his grandson, Randle Wilbraham Falconer, was physician to the Bath hospital, and mayor of the city in 1857; he, too, lived in the Circus, and practised there for more than thirty years.

FIELDING, Henry (1707-1754)
'Fielding's Lodge', Twerton: *Widcombe Lodge

The author of *Tom Jones* lived for some time at Twerton, then near Bath, but now within the city's boundaries. He was there in 1748, and is believed to have written part of his famous novel during that visit. The house, long known as 'Fielding's Lodge', has been demolished, and a small block of flats bearing the defaced legend 'Fielding's House', now stands on the site.

Fielding's sister Sarah was also a novelist, and lived at Widcombe Lodge in the village of Widcombe; like Twerton, it was then near Bath, and is now part of the city. Fielding often stayed with her, and was frequently a guest at Prior Park, Ralph Allen's stately mansion nearby. He was a man who led an indulgent life, and although only in his late thirties at the time, his health was far from good; one of Allen's guests at Prior Park described him unflatteringly as 'a poor, emaciated, worn-out rake, whose gout and infirmities have got the better of his buffoonery'.

Ralph Allen was the model for Squire Allworthy in *Tom Jones,* and Sophia, the heroine, is said to have been inspired by Fielding's first wife, Charlotte, whose early death caused him prolonged grief. He sold the copyright of the novel outright to a publisher for £600. Later, his work as a London magistrate claimed much of his time and energy, and his health declined to such an extent that he was advised to live in a warmer climate. In the spring of 1754 he sailed with his wife and family to Lisbon, hoping to assuage the miseries of his gout, jaundice and asthma. Two months later, at the age of forty-seven, he died, and was buried among the cypresses of the English cemetery in Portugal's capital.

Tom Jones is happily still in print, and continues to delight readers after more than two hundred years. And the reputation of the 'poor, emaciated, worn-out rake' is

Edmund Burke—portrait by an artist of the Reynolds studio.

Frances D'Arblay—portrait by E. F. Burney.

Charles Dickens—portrait by S. Laurence.

Thomas Gainsborough—portrait by Zoffany.

Edward Gibbon—portrait by Henry Walton.

Oliver Goldsmith—portrait by an artist of the Reynolds studio.

George Frederick Handel—portrait by T. Hudson.

Sir William Herschel—portrait by L. F. Abbott.

fittingly enshrined in the more charitable words of a later voluptuary; he was, said Byron, 'the prose Homer of human nature'. A bronze tablet at Widcombe Lodge records the fact that Sarah and Henry Fielding stayed there. It was unveiled by Sir Arthur Conan Doyle in June, 1906.

FIELDING, Sarah (1710-1768)
Widcombe Lodge

Sarah Fielding lived for a time at Widcombe Lodge, Bath. Like her celebrated brother Henry Fielding, she wrote novels, the best known of which was *The Adventures of David Simple*. She was also a pioneer in the field of children's fiction, at a time when this particular *genre* was virtually unknown. Ralph Allen, who lived at Prior Park nearby, encouraged her greatly, and left her £100 in his will. Henry Fielding stayed at Widcombe Lodge several times and, with his sister, often visited Allen at Prior Park. There is a bronze tablet on the Lodge, commemorating both authors; it was unveiled by Sir Arthur Conan Doyle in June, 1906.

FITZHERBERT, Maria Anne (1756-1837)
27 Great Pulteney Street

When he was Prince of Wales, George IV was infatuated with Mrs. Fitzherbert. She was a Roman Catholic, and had been twice married and widowed when, in December 1785, they secretly married. But legally the marriage was invalid. The Act of Settlement decreed that if an heir apparent

33

married a Roman Catholic, he forfeited all right to the crown; and the Marriage Act stated that any member of the royal family who wished to marry under the age of twenty-five, could only do so with the King's consent—and George III would never have given that. Nevertheless, the Prince and his morganatic wife lived together for nearly twenty years, and when they finally separated, Mrs. Fitzherbert was given a generous pension of £6,000 a year — probably in excess of £50,000 by today's standards. George was undoubtedly devoted to her although never, of course, faithful; when he died in 1830, he was wearing a miniature portrait of her round his neck.

Mrs. Fitzherbert came to Bath in 1788-89, to stay with her mother, Mrs. Smythe, at No. 27 Great Pulteney Street.

FREDERICK AUGUSTUS, Duke of York
(1763-1827)
1 and 16 Royal Crescent

George III's second son, Frederick Augustus, Duke of York, enjoys a modest measure of immortality because he inspired a nursery rhyme:

> 'The grand old Duke of York
> He had ten thousand men;
> He marched them up to the top of a hill,
> And he marched them down again'.

After an undistinguished military career he became commander-in-chief of the army, and was involved in an unsavoury scandal when his mistress, Mrs. Mary Anne Clarke, was accused of taking bribes to procure—through the Duke— promotions for senior army officers. He was eventually exonerated, but relieved of his command for two years. Nevertheless, he did much to improve the army's standards of efficiency.

He visited Bath in 1795, when he attended the opening of the new Pump Room, and was presented with the Freedom of the city. In the following year he stayed at No. 1 Royal Crescent; the *Bath Chronicle* announced that 'the Duke of York has engaged the first house in the Crescent, late Mr. Sandford's, as his residence'.

On subsequent visits the Duke lodged at No. 16 Royal Crescent, now part of the Royal Crescent Hotel, where a suite has been named after him. Like his brother the Prince Regent, later George IV, he was a man who loved the good things of life, and he would certainly have enjoyed the luxury of the modern accommodation that bears his name. His coat-of-arms can be seen over the archway at the east end of Northumberland Place.

FRERE, Sir Bartle (1815-1884)
8 Norfolk Buildings

Born in the year of Waterloo, and educated at Bath Grammar School and Haileybury, Bartle Frere emerged as one of the great proconsuls of the nineteenth century, becoming successively Commissioner of Sind, Governor of Bombay, and the first High Commissioner of South Africa. 'The conception of Empire was the keynote of his policy from first to last', wrote a contemporary historian. As a boy in Bath he lived at No. 8 Norfolk Buildings, and in 1830 saw Princess Victoria open the new Victoria Park; nearly thirty years later, as Queen Victoria, she awarded him the KCB, following his service in India at the time of the mutiny. In 1880 he was recalled from his post as High Commissioner of

South Africa, on the grounds that he had superseded his instructions, and was censured by the government. He died four years later, and was buried in St. Paul's. In 1888 his statue on the Thames Embankment was unveiled by the Prince of Wales.

A bronze tablet commemorating his early days at No. 8 Norfolk Buildings, has been removed.

FRIESE-GREEN, William (1855-1921)
*23 Gay Street; *9 The Corridor*

The cinema owes much to Friese-Green. He was the first man to produce sensitized celluloid ribbon suitable as a negative base, and thus to make moving pictures possible. He was born in Bristol and, after serving his apprenticeship as a photographer, he came to Bath and opened a studio at No. 23 Gay Street, later moving to No. 9 the Corridor. Whilst in Bath he met John Arthur Rudge, who was a native of the city, and who lived in New Bond Street Place. Rudge had been experimenting with the technique of producing moving pictures by means of separate photographs mounted on a revolving drum; and their partnership opened the way for the invention of the first movie camera. Friese-Green prospered, and opened studios in London, at No. 69 New Bond Street, and in Plymouth and Bristol. He died in London in 1921, and is buried in Highgate Cemetery. Sir Edwin Lutyens designed his tomb.

In New Bond Street Place, a bronze tablet commemorates his achievement, and that of his colleague and friend, John Arthur Rudge.

GAINSBOROUGH, Thomas (1727-1788)
17 the Circus

Gainsborough came to Bath from Ipswich at the instigation, it is said, of the eccentric Philip Thicknesse— although the fact that his sister, Mrs. Mary Gibbon, kept a lodging house in the city, close to Abbey Churchyard, may well have influenced his decision. He stayed at Mrs. Gibbon's home after his arrival in Bath, using a room facing the south-west door of the abbey as a studio.

At that time visiting artists were invited to display their work in the Pump Room, with their scale of charges, and Gainsborough took prompt advantage of this facility. The quality of his work was quickly recognised, and commissions for portraits began to flow in. During his first months in the city he charged five guineas for a portrait, and as he became established, he increased the rate to a hundred guineas for a full-length portrait, forty guineas for a half-length, and five guineas for a head. Soon he was ready to move to more commodious premises, and late in 1763 he wrote to his friend James Unwin: 'I have taken a house about three-quarters of a mile in the Lansdown Road: it is sweetly situated, and I have every convenience I could wish for. I pay thirty pounds a year . . .' Three years later he felt confident enough to move to the Circus, and to rent one of the newly-completed houses there, at two hundred guineas a year.

The houses in the Circus were not numbered at that time, and Gainsborough always gave his address simply as 'Mr. Gainsborough, Bath'. It was originally thought that his house was No. 24, and in June 1902 a bronze tablet was unveiled there by Sir Walter Armstrong, a noted authority on the painter's work. But after detailed research into the rate books of the period, it was proved that the house he rented was No. 17; and late in 1971 the plaque was transferred to its present position.

During the years he spent in Bath, Gainsborough painted the portraits of Lord Chesterfield, Garrick, Sterne, Richardson, Sheridan, Burke, James Quin, Elizabeth Linley and many others. One of his most famous paintings, *The Blue Boy,* was probably completed during his stay in the city, and clearly reflects his admiration for Van Dyck. The model for the portrait was Jonathan Buttall, the son of one of Gainsborough's friends who was a prosperous ironmonger in London's Soho.

Gainsborough left Bath in 1774 after a quarrel with Thicknesse, and settled in London, where his work continued to attract fashionable patronage. He died in 1788, after contracting a chill at the trial of Warren Hastings which developed into a cancerous tumour of the neck. His last words were 'We are going to Heaven, and Van Dyck is of the company'.

GARRICK, David (1717 – 1779)
North Parade

When he was twenty-four, Garrick appeared as Richard III in London, and transformed the whole concept of acting as it then was. Instead of performing in the stilted, artificial style that was customary at the time, he played the part in a completely realistic manner, devoid of affectation, that astonished everyone who saw him. Quin, one of the outstanding performers of the day, was moved to remark "If the young fellow is right, I and the rest of the players have been all wrong". Soon afterwards, he was engaged by the management of Drury Lane at an unprecedented salary, and went on to establish himself as one of the greatest actors of the eighteenth century, and to become a household name in the long annals of the English stage.

He never acted in the Bath theatre, but he visited the city at least four times, chiefly to take the waters. He came in 1745 and 1751, staying at Mrs. White's lodging establishment on North Parade. In the winter of 1766 he returned for a few days: his fellow-actor and admirer Quin, who lived in Bath, had died, and Garrick wrote the epitaph that is inscribed on his memorial tablet in the Abbey – a tribute that begins with an oft-quoted couplet:

> "That Tongue which set the Table in a roar
> And charmed the public ear, is heard no more . . ."

His last visit to Bath was in 1770, nine years before he died. After his burial in Westminster Abbey, Dr. Johnson remarked that his passing had "eclipsed the gaiety of nations".

GIBBON, Edward (1739-1794)
8 Belvedere; 22 Charles Street

In 1764 Gibbon went on a tour of Italy, and while 'musing amidst the ruins of the Capitol' in Rome, he conceived the idea of 'writing the decline and fall of the city'. The first volume of *The Decline and Fall of the Roman Empire* was published in 1776, and the work was completed twelve years later, in 1788. Since then it has achieved the status of a masterpiece.

Gibbon presented a copy of the first volume to the Duke of Gloucester, brother of George III, and made a similar gesture when the second volume appeared. The Duke laid the quarto on a table and remarked affably, 'Another damn'd thick, square book! Always scribble, scribble, scribble! Eh! Mr. Gibbon?' The work, nevertheless, made an immediate impact, and ensured Gibbon's place in the pantheon of great historical writers. He earned £6,000 for writing it, and the booksellers netted £60,000 for printing it.

He was a short man, less than five feet tall, and he was often mocked because of his plump, squat appearance. Much of his life was spent in Lausanne, but he was a frequent visitor to Bath, where he stayed with his step-mother at No. 8 Belvedere (on Lansdown Road) and No. 22 Charles Street. He admired the city a great deal, and in July 1789 he wrote from Switzerland to his friend Lord Sheffield: 'I am still deeply rooted in this country . . . yet in England, when the present clouds are dispelled, I could form a very comfortable establishment in London, or rather at Bath'. He returned to England in 1793, but died within a year, of a long-standing complaint that he had criminally neglected for thirty years.

GILBERT, Marie Dolores Eliza, Countess of Lansfeldt, known as Lola Montez (1818-1861)
53 Great Pulteney Street

Lola Montez, one of the most notorious adventuresses of the nineteenth century, came to Bath as a young girl to advance her education, and stayed at No. 53 Great Pulteney Street. Within a comparatively short time, her worldly knowledge had advanced to such an extent that she felt able to elope from Bath with a Captain James of the Indian army. Eventually they were married; but Lola soon embarked on a career as a Spanish dancer, appearing at theatres and elsewhere in Germany, Russia, Poland and Bavaria, and meeting Alexander Dumas in Paris. Nicholas, the Czar of Russia, showered her with expensive gifts, and King Ludwig of Bavaria became completely infatuated with her; he gave her a pension of 20,000 florins and a superb mansion, and created her Countess of Lansfeldt. In 1849, when she was thirty-one, she married George Heald in London, and was promptly summoned for bigamy. She fled to Spain to evade the legal consequences, and then appeared in America as a dancer, where she married a newspaper tycoon named P. P. Hull, although she already had two husbands still living. She ended her eventful life in New York, full of penitence, embracing Methodism, and caring for the needy.

GOLDSMITH, Oliver (1728-1774)
11 North Parade

The author of *The Vicar of Wakefield*, Dr. Johnson tells us, came to Bath in 1771 with his patron, Lord Clare. He probably stayed at No. 11 North Parade on that occasion, the house in which Edmund Burke lived just before his death thirty-six years later; there is a bronze tablet on the façade to record Goldsmith's visit. But he also came to Bath in 1762, the year in which he published his *Citizen of the World*. Beau Nash had just died, and he saw an opportunity to produce a topical biography that would bring him some financial reward. He was often in difficulty over money; *The Vicar of Wakefield* was completed in 1766, and Johnson arranged its sale with a publisher for £60, thus enabling the struggling Goldsmith to settle the arrears of his rent.

His biography of Nash was characteristically frank, and made no attempt to whitewash the old autocrat. 'He went to the very summit of second-rate luxury' Goldsmith wrote; and of the Beau's wit, he said 'Of all the jests recorded of him, I scarce find one that is not marked with petulance . . . once a week he might say a good thing'. The book contains an admirably perceptive assessment of Bath's popularity at that time: 'Bath came into vogue because people of fashion

41

had no agreeable summer retreat from London, and usually spent that season amidst a solitude of country squires and parson's wives and visiting tenant farmers. They wanted some place where they might have each other's company and win each other's money, as they had done during the winter in town'.

Goldsmith died at the early age of forty-six, after a short illness. He is buried in the Temple Church, London.

HAMILTON, Emma, Lady (1765-1815)
6 Edward Street

It is often suggested that Nelson's great love was in Bath when he was convalescing at No. 2 Pierrepont Street. That was in 1781 and Emma Lyon, as she was then, is said to have been a maidservant in the Linley household at No. 1 Pierrepont Place, just across the street. It is a nice story, but the evidence for it is threadbare—as it is for the claim that she stayed in Bath in 1798; in that year, as Lady Hamilton, she was busy entertaining Nelson in Naples, after his great victory in the battle of the Nile, and there are no indications that she visited England.

It seems likely, however, that she came to Bath after Nelson's death. Three or four years after Trafalgar, she is said to have lived for a time at No. 6 Edward Street. She had squandered most of the generous legacies left her by Nelson and Sir William Hamilton, and was rapidly approaching penury. Later she spent thirteen months in a debtors' prison, and died in obscurity at Calais in 1815.

HANDEL, George Frederic (1685-1758)
3 Pierrepont Street

Rather surprisingly perhaps, Handel was a close friend of James Quin, the actor and wit who often referred to Bath as 'a fine slope to the grave', and said that he 'did not know a better place for an old cock to roost in'. It was Quin who persuaded the composer to visit Bath with him in 1749, in order that he might benefit from the waters; he probably lodged with Quin at the actor's house, No. 3 Pierrepont Street. Handel returned the following year, and in 1751 he came again to the city with his devoted secretary, John Christopher Smith. The waters gave him only temporary relief from his rheumatism, and he was now facing the onset of blindness; he was not present when his oratorio *Messiah* was first performed in Bath in 1755, at Wiltshire's Rooms near the Parades. He planned a further visit to the city in 1759, but worsening health prevented his travelling, and he died only a week after cancelling his arrangements. Smith continued his work on Handel's behalf, and came to live in Bath after his retirement in 1774, at No. 18 Brock Street.

HARGOOD, Admiral Sir William (1762-1839)
9 Royal Crescent

Admiral Hargood retired to Bath after a distinguished naval career that spanned almost sixty years, and lived at No. 9 Royal Crescent from 1834 until his death in 1839. At the time of Trafalgar he was a captain commanding the *Belleisle*, a 74-gun ship-of-the-line under Nelson's flag.

Hargood was promoted admiral on July 22nd 1831, and two months later, on the occasion of William IV's coronation, he was awarded the KCB. He had served as a lieutenant with the King—then Prince William Henry—on the frigate *Hebe* in 1785, and afterwards they had corresponded regularly; the award was a gesture of friendship from one old salt to another, but richly deserved, nonetheless. After a three-year spell as commander-in-chief at Plymouth, Sir William spent five years of retirement in Bath, and died at No. 9 Royal Crescent on 11th September, 1839. He was buried in Bath Abbey, and his portrait hangs in the famous Painted Hall at Greenwich.

HARRISON, Frederic (1829-1923)
10 Royal Crescent

Frederic Harrison came to live at No. 10 Royal Crescent in 1912, when he was eighty-three years old, and after a long life devoted to public service and writing.

He was the son of a prosperous London merchant whose country residence was Sutton Place near Guildford, the impressive mansion that was later to become the home of millionaire Paul Getty. After being called to the Bar, he practised as a lawyer for fifteen years, and then devoted much of his life to writing. His religious beliefs were centred on the doctrine of positivism, which recognises only matters of fact and experience; it has been defined, perhaps more explicitly, as a 'reorganisation of life, at once intellectual, moral and social, by faith in our common humanity'.

Harrison loved Bath, and praised the city wholeheartedly in an article he wrote for *Blackwood's Magazine.* 'Here are the most important Roman buildings in our island;' he wrote, 'one of our great medieval cathedrals; the best English examples of Palladian architecture adapted to city planning; a river valley that may hold its own beside the

44

Thames at Marlow, and downs that may challenge the racecourse at Goodwood'.

On his ninetieth birthday in 1919, he was paid a remarkable tribute. An appreciative address was presented to him in his library at No. 10 the Crescent—signed by the Prime Minister, Mr. Lloyd George, the leaders of both the Liberal and Labour parties, the bishops of London and Exeter, and many prominent doctors, authors, journalists, artists and musicians. There were ninety signatures on the address—one for every year of his life. A month later Bath endorsed the tribute by presenting him with the Freedom of the city. His long, immensely productive life ended peacefully in January, 1923.

HAYDN, Franz Joseph (1732-1809)
Perrymead Villa, Lyncombe

Haydn composed more than a hundred symphonies and concertos and of these, twelve symphonies were written in England, on visits he made in 1791 and 1784. On his second visit in 1794, he spent three pleasant days with Venanzio Rauzzini, Bath's musical director, at the impressario's country retreat at Perrymead, Lyncombe. The composer noted in his diary on August 8th 1794: 'Lodged at Mr. V. Rauzzini's, musician'; and the *Bath Chronicle,* on the same day, recorded his name under the heading 'Arrived here'.

Rauzzini had buried a much-loved pet, his dog Turk, in the garden, with an inscribed stone over the grave. Haydn was so touched by this that he set part of the inscription to music as a round, or canon, for four voices.

HAYGARTH, Dr. John (1740-1827)
15 Royal Crescent

In 1798 a distinguished physician took up residence at No. 15 Royal Crescent, next door to the centre house. He was Dr. John Haygarth, and he occupied the house for two years. For more than thirty years before that he had served as physician to Chester Infirmary, and he was in his late fifties when he came to Bath.

In those days the attention paid in hospital to such elementary precautions as isolation, ventilation and scrupulous cleanliness was negligible. John Haygarth was the first English doctor to appreciate their crucial importance, and to apply them rigorously. He conceived the idea, which is now universal, of separately treating fever patients in isolated wards, and Chester Infirmary adopted the principle in 1783. It seems incredible to us now, when we take hygiene in hospitals for granted, that these basic health requirements were hardly recognised two hundred years ago. Dr. Haygarth was a pioneer in their implementation, and he is remembered in medical history for the vital contribution he made to the advancement of public health.

HERSCHEL, Sir William (1738-1822)
*19 New King Street

'I have looked further into space than ever a human being did before me'. This was the proud boast of William Herschel, a German military bandsman who left Hanover for England in 1757, made a very good living for himself as a musician in Bath and then, as a self-taught astronomer, discovered a new planet, Uranus.

Herschel came to Bath in 1766. He was a good enough musician to be appointed organist at the new Octagon Chapel in the city, and later to become musical director at the Assembly Rooms. But his first love was astronomy. With his sister Caroline, he began to make observations of the night sky with a hired telescope. Later, he made his own instruments, devoting every minute of his spare time to the exacting science; and in March 1781, he made his famous sighting of Uranus. He was elected to the Royal Society the same year, and in 1782 he left Bath to take up the prestigious post of Astronomer Royal. He was knighted in 1816.

His final years in Bath were spent at No. 19 New King Street; he was certainly there when he made the unique discovery that crowned his work as an astronomer. Today the building houses a small museum that honours his achievement; and the bronze tablet that adorns the façade has the distinction of being the first of these useful appendages to be sited in the city. It was unveiled in 1898.

HOARE, Prince (1755-1834)
5 Princes Buildings, George Street

Like his father, William Hoare, Prince Hoare studied painting in Rome; but although he exhibited several times at the Royal Academy, failing health persuaded him to turn to authorship, and he wrote a number of books and plays. He achieved some distinction as a dramatist, and his best-known play, *No Song, No Supper,* was staged at Drury Lane in 1790. After the death, in 1799, of James Boswell, Dr. Johnson's celebrated biographer, he was elected Secretary for Foreign Correspondence to the Royal Academy. He was born in Bath, and lived for some years at No. 5 Princes Buildings, in George Street.

In an alcove at the east end of the Pump Room stands a statue of Beau Nash, gazing imperiously over the room and its visitors. It was sculpted by another Prince Hoare, the brother of William Hoare, and uncle of the artist and dramatist.

HOARE, William (1707-1792)
6 Edgar Buildings, George Street

Although he was born at Eye in Suffolk, William Hoare lived and worked in Bath for more than fifty years, and was highly regarded as a portrait painter. He came to the city in 1739, and lived at No. 6 Edgar Buildings from 1752 until his death forty years later.

He had studied painting for nine years in Rome, and although his work never commanded the high fees that Gainsborough and Lawrence were able to charge, it nevertheless brought him considerable success and prosperity. He painted Chatham, Beau Nash, Christopher Anstey, John Palmer and several other Bath celebrities; and his crayon portraits of Chesterfield and Pope are to be seen in the National Gallery. His splendid portrait of Anstey hangs in the Guildhall at Bath, and that of Beau Nash can be seen in the Pump Room. Like Gainsborough, he was a founder member of the Royal Academy; and until Gainsborough came to Bath in 1759, he was undoubtedly the city's foremost painter.

Countess Huntingdon—artist unknown.

Samuel Johnson—portrait by Sir Joshua Reynolds.

Walter Savage Landor—portrait by W. Fisher.

Sir Thomas Lawrence—by R. Evans after a self-portrait.

HOOD, Admiral Alexander, Viscount Bridport
(1727-1819)
34 Great Pulteney Street

Alexander Hood was promoted Admiral of the Blue in 1794, and in the same year was second in command to Lord Howe at the famous sea battle against the French that has since been known as the 'Glorious First of June'. Two years later he was Vice-Admiral of England, and was created a viscount in 1801. At the end of his active life he retired to Bath, and lived at No. 34 Great Pulteney Street. He died there in 1819.

He is often confused with his equally distinguished elder brother, Admiral Samuel Hood, who also became a viscount, and who stayed for a time in Bath at No. 5 Queen Square, in 1806-07.

HOWE, Admiral William, Earl Howe (1726-1799)
*71 Great Pulteney Street

Residents in Great Pulteney Street during the last years of the eighteenth century would often have seen a tall, commanding figure in naval uniform walking slowly—sometimes with the aid of crutches—towards the Pump Room. Admiral Howe had retired from the navy, and was taking the Bath waters in an attempt to relieve the pain and discomfort occasioned by gout and rheumatism.

Between 1780 and 1798 he visited the city regularly, sometimes twice a year, and occasionally for months at a time; towards the end of his life he stayed frequently at No. 71 Great Pulteney Street.

His naval career had been a distinguished one, crowned by

a great victory against the French off Ushant in 1794; the culminating day of the battle, on which several French ships were captured and one sunk by gunfire, has gone down in history as the 'Glorious First of June'. National rejoicing over the victory was widespread, and manifested itself in widely varying degrees of exuberance. George III presented Howe with a diamond-hilted sword; and Moses Pickwick, mine host at the *White Hart* in Bath—and the father of the Moses Pickwick who inspired Charles Dickens—displayed a huge painting of the admiral standing on the deck of his ship, the *Queen Charlotte*, with a patriotic, but rather pedestrian couplet underneath:

> 'France may in vain pour forth her cannon balls,
> While gallant Howe commands her wooden walls'.

Later, Howe was promoted Admiral of the Fleet, and awarded the Order of the Garter. He retired from the navy in 1797, and was frequently at Bath before his death in 1799. The bronze tablet on the wall of No. 71 Great Pulteney Street was unveiled by Admiral Jellicoe in 1931—appropriately on the first of June.

HUNTER, John (1728-1793)
12 South Parade

One of the claims advanced on behalf of John Hunter is that he 'advanced surgery as far as it was possible to go before the introduction of anaesthetics in the next (i.e. the nineteenth) century'. Towards the close of the eighteenth century he was widely regarded as the leading surgeon in England; he had been appointed Surgeon Extraordinary to George III in 1776, and among his other lucrative posts was Surgeon General and Inspector General of Hospitals. One of his pupils, who became a close friend, was Edward Jenner, the discoverer of the principle of vaccination against smallpox.

Hunter produced a number of important medical works, and bought land in Leicester Square and Castle Street in London in 1785, to build a large anatomical museum and a workshop for his experiments and dissections. Soon afterwards, he lived for a time in Bath, at No. 12 South Parade, where a bronze tablet records his stay. He died in London in 1793, and was buried at St. Martin's-in-the-Fields; his remains were removed to Westminster Abbey in 1859.

HUNTINGDON, Countess of (1707-1791)
4 Edgar Buildings, George Street

Horace Walpole called her 'the Queen of the Methodists', Whitefield described her as 'all aflame for Jesus', and George III 'wished to God there was a Lady Huntingdon in every diocese of the kingdom'. Selina, Countess of Huntingdon, was one of the earliest converts to the teachings of John Wesley; she built chapels all over the country, appointed her own ministers, and referred to her religious activities as 'The Countess of Huntingdon's Connexion'. Wesley eventually grew tired of her egotism, and complained that she always spoke of '*my* college, *my* masters, *my* students: "I" mixes with everything'. She was a forceful, domineering woman who energetically tried to convert influential people, including Lord Chesterfield and Beau Nash, to the new sect.

She built a chapel in Bath in the Vineyards in 1765, and the following year Horace Walpole, staying at Chapel Court, went there to hear Wesley preach; afterwards, he wrote to a friend: 'My health advances faster than my amusement.

However, I have been at one opera, Mr. Wesley's. The chapel is very neat, with true Gothic windows (yet I am not converted); but I was glad to see that luxury was creeping in upon them before persecution'. In 1932 the chapel became Presbyterian, and from 1972 a United Reform Church. Selina sometimes lived in the house attached to it, but her chief residence in Bath was No. 4 Edgar Buildings, at the top of Milsom Street.

JAY, Rev. William (1769-1853)
Argyle Street Chapel

There cannot be many churches or chapels in the United Kingdom that can claim to have had the same minister for more than sixty years. At Argyle Street Chapel in Bath, William Jay was ordained as pastor in 1791, as a young man of twenty-two, and preached his last sermon there in August, 1852—an impressive span of sixty-one years that justifiably earned him the bronze tablet on the chapel's façade (although the dates it carries are slightly erroneous).

Jay was held in the greatest esteem throughout this long period. On his completing fifty years as minister, a public breakfast was held in his honour, attended by eight hundred guests; and he was presented with a silver salver, and a purse containing the generous sum of £650. Wilberforce, Beckford and Carlyle all admired him as a preacher, and Sheridan declared him to be 'the most manly orator he had ever heard'. He died only a year after retiring, at the age of eighty-four.

JERVIS, John, Earl St. Vincent (1735-1823)
8 Argyle Street

When he defeated the Spanish fleet off Cape St. Vincent on 16th February 1797, Admiral Jervis was awarded a pension of £3,000, given the Freedom of the city of London, and created Earl St. Vincent. It was the apogee of a distinguished naval career that spanned more than fifty years, and culminated in his appointment as First Lord of the Admiralty and Admiral of the Fleet.

In 1759, when he was twenty-four, he led the squadron that escorted General Wolfe's troops to Canada; and just before Wolfe died on the Heights of Abraham at Quebec, he entrusted Jervis with his last message to his fiancée, Miss Lowther of Bath. The admiral came to Bath several times in later years with his sister, and lodged at No. 8 Argyle Street.

JOHNSON, Samuel (1709-1784)
Pelican Inn, Walcot Street (now demolished)

The great lexicographer and essayist, immortalised in Boswell's famous biography, was one of the major literary figures of the late eighteenth century. He came to Bath in the spring of 1776, travelling with Henry Thrale to join Thrale's wife and daughter in the city. The journey, by diligence, took seventeen hours, with stops at the Castle Inn, Marlborough, and the Black Bear at Devizes.

The season in Bath at that time was a particularly brilliant one. Sheridan's *The Rivals* was playing to crowded houses at the Orchard Street Theatre, Herschel was playing in the Pump Room band, and the Parades were thronged with distinguished visitors. Johnson was officially welcomed by the Corporation, and lionised throughout his stay; he visited Dr. Nugent in the Circus, whose daughter had married Edmund Burke, called on Mrs. Thrale who was staying in North Parade, and was a welcome guest at Prior Park, the former home of Ralph Allen. He was well aware of the city's benevolent qualities, as he proved later when he replied to a lady who had written to him to tell him how unhappy she was: 'Let me counsel you not to waste your health in unprofitable sorrow, but go to Bath and endeavour to prolong your life'.

He lodged at the Pelican Inn at Walcot Street, a hostelry with a spacious courtyard and a pleasant garden running down to the River Avon. The inn later became known as 'The Three Cups', and was eventually demolished to make way for part of the Beaufort Hotel complex. In February 1923, G. K. Chesterton unveiled a bronze tablet on "The Three Cups" to commemorate Johnson's visit.

KNIGHT, Henrietta, Lady Luxborough (d. 1756)
Orange Grove

In January 1752 Lady Luxborough, a half-sister of Henry St. John, Viscount Bolingbroke, came to Bath to take a course of the waters. She lodged with a Mrs. Hodgkinson in Orange Grove and stayed in the city for three months, visiting the King's Bath each day, and dutifully taking the three glasses of Bath water daily that Dr. Oliver prescribed for her. The treatment improved her health; and in a series of letters to her close friend, the poet William Shenstone, she amusingly described the attractions that the city offered. 'Would you see the fortunate and benevolent Mr. Allen, his fine house and his stone quarries?' she wrote,
54

'Would you see our law-giver, Mr. Nash, whose white hat commands more respect and non-resistance than the Crowns of some Kings, though now worn on a head that is in the eightieth year of its age? . . . Hasten, then, your steps; for he may soon be carried off the stage of life, as the greatest must fall to the worm's repast'.

Shenstone resisted the inducement to join her, but she continued to enthuse about the city's appeal. She greatly enjoyed the music in the Pump Room, and visited the new Orchard Street theatre, which had been opened about a year previously. And Ralph Allen invited her to Prior Park, where she met Lady Huntingdon, William Hoare, Sarah Fielding, Dr. Oliver and the elder John Wood. Allen, she noted, spent much time chatting to Wood and Dr. Oliver about plans for the new grammar school to be built in Broad Street.

Horace Walpole, that inveterate eighteenth-century gossip, described Lady Luxborough in one of his letters as 'high-coloured and lusty', with 'a great black bush of hair'. On her own evidence, she enjoyed her stay in Bath immensely, although the improvement in her health was comparatively short-lived; she died four years later, in 1756.

LAMBALLE, Marie Thérèse, Princesse de (1749-1792)
1 Royal Crescent

In 1786 an important visitor from France lodged at No. 1 Royal Crescent. She was Marie Thérèse Louise de Savoie Carignon, Princesse de Lamballe, friend and lady-in-waiting to Queen Marie-Antoinette. According to the *Bath Chronicle* of 27th September 1786, she arrived with a large retinue of servants, and her personal physician. She was a pale, slim lady with curly, fair hair and a prominent nose. She was abnormally sensitive; if she suffered the slightest shock, she would collapse into a faint that often lasted for two hours. The smell of violets made her disastrously ill, and the sight of shellfish, even in a painting, sent her into a nervous fit.

She came back to England in 1791, when the French Revolution was at its height, hoping to persuade the British royal family to help Louis XVI and Marie-Antoinette to escape from France. But when she returned to Paris she died horribly, as the Revolution reached its bloody climax in the September Massacres of 1782.

LANDOR, Walter Savage (1775-1864)
35 St. James's Square; 3 Rivers Street

'Bath has no resemblance on earth, and I have never been happy in any other place long together'. These laudatory words were written by the poet and prose writer Walter Savage Landor, who lived in the city for twenty years—after spending fourteen years in Florence.

He was an ebullient character, impulsive and occasionally arrogant. Visiting Bath for the first time in 1811, he saw an attractive girl at a ball, quickly obtained an introduction, and within a very short time had married her. They lived in Florence, and there Landor wrote *Imaginary Conversations,* the prose work by which he is best known. But his relationship with his wife was a stormy one, and in 1837 he came to Bath alone, eventually taking a house at No. 35 St. James's Square. Here he entertained Dickens and Carlyle. Dickens conceived the character of *Little Nell* whilst staying with Landor, and Carlyle, when he visited the house in 1850, was enchanted with Bath. He thought it 'the prettiest town in all England'; and then, for a Scot, he bestowed the ultimate accolade on the city: 'Nay, Edinburgh itself, except for the sea and the Grampians, does not equal it'.

Towards the end of his two decades in Bath, Landor lived for six years at No. 3 Rivers Street. His longest tenancy, however, was in No. 35 St. James's Square, and it is here that a bronze tablet records his association with the city. He returned to Florence—with which he frequently compared Bath—and died there in 1864. The quatrain he wrote, brusquely entitled *Finis,* could well serve as his epitaph:

'I strove with none, for none was worth my strife;
Nature I loved and, next to Nature, Art;
I warm'd my hands before the fire of life;
It sinks, and I am ready to depart'.

LAWRENCE, Sir Thomas (1769-1830)
2 Alfred Street

Among the many portrait painters of his day, Lawrence was pre-eminent; he was a President of the Royal Academy, succeeded Reynolds as official portrait painter to King George III, and played a significant part in the founding of the National Portrait Gallery. After receiving his knighthood in 1815, he travelled in Europe, fulfilling many commissions to paint political and military leaders, and extending his already wide reputation considerably.

His father was an innkeeper who kept the old Bear Hotel in the market place at Devizes. Young Lawrence drew portraits of the inn's customers, and achieved a measure of local fame. By the time the family moved to Bath in 1780, taking a house at No. 2 Alfred Street, he was making a useful income; before he was even twelve years old, his studio in Alfred Street was attracting fashionable and influential patrons from the city and elsewhere. He left Bath when he was eighteen, and became a student at the Royal

Academy schools in London; and so rapid was his progress that only five years were to pass before his appointment as official portrait painter to the King was confirmed. He died in 1830, and was buried in St. Paul's Cathedral.

LEIGHTON, Frederic, Lord Leighton (1830-1896)
9 the Circus

Among the numerous English painters of the nineteenth century, Frederic Leighton was outstanding. He studied at Florence, and his first major work, *Cimabue's 'Madonna' carried in Procession*, was exhibited at the Royal Academy in 1855, and bought by Queen Victoria. He opposed pre-Raphaelite romantic realism, and adopted pseudo-Hellenistic classicism as his *métier; The Captive Andromache*, exhibited at the Royal Academy in 1885, is a perfect example of his style. He was President of the Royal Academy from 1878 until 1896, was knighted in 1878, and raised to the peerage the day before his death in 1896.

His father was a doctor who practised at No. 9 the Circus for some time, and Leighton visited his parents here on several occasions; his name and achievements are inscribed on their tomb in Locksbrook Cemetery, Lower Weston. During many of his productive years as a painter, he lived at Holland Park House, Kensington. He was buried in St. Paul's Cathedral.

LINLEY, Elizabeth (later Mrs. Sheridan)
(1754-1792)
*Pierrepont Place; *11 Royal Crescent

She was beautiful, and she sang like an angel. Gainsborough and Reynolds painted her portrait; two men fought duels over her; and George III, if we are to believe Horace Walpole, 'ogled her at an oratorio'.

Elizabeth Linley was a member of a very talented musical family. Her father, Thomas Linley, arranged concerts in Bath, gave music lessons, and played the harpsichord expertly. Thomas, her brother, was an accomplished violinist who visited Italy as a child prodigy, and won the friendship and approbation of Mozart: he died tragically in a boating accident when he was twenty-two. And Mary, her sister, was also a talented singer. The family had lived in Bath for many years—first at Abbey Green, then at Pierrepont Place, close to the Doric archway that links Orchard Street and Pierrepont Street (there is a bronze tablet here), and finally at No. 11 Royal Crescent.

Elizabeth's beauty naturally attracted several suitors. But eventually two men emerged as chief contenders in the inevitable race for her favours. One was Richard Brinsley Sheridan, the future playwright, whose father taught elocution in Bath; the other was a married man, Captain Thomas Mathews. Sheridan showed his resourcefulness by persuading the lady to elope with him to France from No. 11 the Crescent; but when they returned to England, Captain Mathews was simmering with hostility, and lost no time in publishing a strongly-worded attack on Sheridan in the *Bath Chronicle*. The two men fought twice with swords, in London and at Kingsdown near Bath, and in the second encounter Sheridan was seriously wounded.

The passionate scenario appeared to have a happy ending when Elizabeth ultimately married Sheridan at Marylebone

Church in 1773. But two or three years later, the embryo playwright emerged into the limelight; his two great comedies, *The Rivals* and *The School for Scandal*, were staged successfully, and he became the proprietor of the Drury Lane theatre. Later, he was elected MP for Stafford, and achieved some notoriety as a politician and a close friend of the Prince of Wales. Poor Elizabeth found it difficult to cope with her changed circumstances, and with Sheridan's infidelity. She contracted tuberculosis and died in 1792, at the tragically early age of thirty-eight.

The bronze tablet on the façade of No. 11 Royal Crescent commemorates her famous elopement in 1772.

LIVINGSTONE, David (1813-1873)
13 the Circus

When, in September 1864, the famous explorer came to Bath to address the British Association, he stayed at No. 13 the Circus. The meeting was held in the Theatre Royal, and the crowded audience, to quote the words of a local reporter, 'presented quite an array of science and learning'. After he had been enthusiastically welcomed, Livingstone spoke at length of his travels in Africa. The famous occasion when he was rescued by Stanley occurred eight years later, in 1872, at the climax of a dangerous and harrowing expedition into the African interior. He died a year later, and was buried in Westminster Abbey.

LOUIS XVIII, King of France (1755-1824)
72 Great Pulteney Street

Louis XVIII was a brother of the ill-fated Louis XVI, who died by the guillotine in 1793. He assumed the title of King in 1795, immediately after the death of the Dauphin; but, as the Comte de Provence, he wandered around Europe for nineteen years, until he was finally proclaimed in 1814.

He came to Bath in August 1813, accompanied by his niece, Marie Thérèse, Duchesse of Angoulême, who was a daughter of Louis XVI and Marie Antoinette. They stayed at 72 Great Pulteney Street, and apparently they were well received in the city; when they left, they were presented with an address, to which Louis replied from his Pulteney Street window. A year later, corpulent and gouty, he became King of France, and died in 1824.

LUNN, Sally
North Parade Passage

'Sally Lunn', wrote Dickens in a nineteenth-century weekly journal, 'the illustrious author of a tea-cake, lived at the close of the last century. Her home was at Bath, where she cried her bun cakes morning and evening about the streets, carrying them in a basket with a white cloth over it'.

Sally lived in what is claimed to be the oldest house in Bath, in North Parade Passage. The plaque on the façade proclaims that it dates from 1482; but at that time the ground on which the house stands was part of the Abbey precinct, and no domestic dwellings would have been built there. Architectural authorities believe that a more acceptable date would be soon after 1539. It is said that two Dukes of Kingston lived there, and that Ralph Allen established his first post office in the house in 1725; but no evidence exists to suggest that Sally lived and worked there, apart from recipes for the cakes which were eventually found in a bake-house oven in the cellar. She is

61

believed to have acquired the house in 1680, but no records substantiate this, or confirm either her birth or death. It is possible that she may be a legendary figure. But the delicious tea-cakes associated with her name can still be enjoyed in the house in North Parade Passage. Legendary or not, her reputation as a Bath character is still very much alive.

LYTTON, Edward Bulwer-, 1st Baron Lytton (1803-1873)
2 Great Pulteney Street; 9 Royal Crescent

Lord Bulwer-Lytton, the nineteenth-century novelist and dramatist, stayed at Bath on several occasions during his later life. He was at No. 9 Royal Crescent in 1866, the year in which he was created a peer; his celebrated novel, *The Last Days of Pompeii*, had been published thirty years previously. The following year, 1867, he transferred his allegiance to No. 2 Great Pulteney Street, which was then Stead's Hotel; there is a bronze tablet on the wall commemorating his visits. He returned to Stead's often during the few years preceding his death, and wrote his last novel, *The Parisians*, there.

In addition to his considerable literary output, Lytton served as a member of parliament for fifteen years, and was colonial secretary in 1858-59. His historical novels, although inclined to be rather heavy, found a wide public in Victorian England. He was friendly with Dickens, who assisted in the production of his play, *Not So Bad As We Seem*, when it was staged at the Assembly Rooms in Bath.

MACAULAY, Mrs. Catharine (1731-1791)
2 Alfred Street

Like her more illustrious namesake, Mrs. Macaulay was a historian; she wrote an eight-volume history of England 'from the accession of James I to that of the Brunswick Line', and settled in Bath when she had almost completed it, in 1774. Her husband had died, and she took rooms in a house at No. 2 Alfred Street, afterwards occupied by the family of Sir Thomas Lawrence; and here she expounded her radical political views, and captivated the owner of the house, a cleric called Dr. Wilson, who erected a statue in her honour in his London church, and presented her with a gold medal. Another gentleman who succumbed to her charms was a Bath quack called Dr. Graham, who later became notorious in London when he exhibited a 'celestial bed' which, he claimed, would 'electrify' any ladies and gentlemen who spent a night in it. To the chagrin of both men, Mrs. Macaulay married William Graham, a younger brother of Dr. Graham, in 1778. Dr. Wilson was so affronted that he tore down the statue in his London church, and sold the vault that he had reserved for her mortal remains.

MALTHUS, Thomas Robert (1766-1834)
17 Portland Place

His *Essay on Population* was published anonymously in 1798, and within a little more than two decades, six editions had appeared. In them, the shrewd political economist developed his view that population, if allowed to expand unchecked, would eventually be reduced by famine, pestilence and war; only vice, misery and self-restraint (by which he meant the deliberate limiting of poor families) would prevent this from happening. His theories were considered by many to be heretical at the time, but are now widely accepted.

After holding a curacy in Surrey for several years, he married a Miss Harriet Eckersall from Bath in 1804, and soon afterwards obtained a post at Haileybury School, where he taught history and political economy. Late in his life he lived at No. 17 Portland Place, Bath, where he died in 1834.

MENUHIN, Yehudi (1916-
Lansdown Grove Hotel

As a child, Yehudi Menuhin was one of the most remarkable prodigies that the twentieth century has produced. He made his public début, as a violinist with an orchestra at San Francisco, when he was seven years old. In Berlin in 1928, when he was only twelve, he played three concertos by Bach, Beethoven and Brahms before the musical élite of Europe. Bruno Walter conducted the orchestra, and Einstein and Kreisler were among the distinguished audience; at the end of the concert Einstein dashed up to Menuhin in the artists' room, hugged him and exclaimed 'Now I know there is a God in heaven!'. And in 1932, at a memorable concert in the Albert Hall—he was sixteen by then—he performed concertos by Bach and Mozart under the baton of Sir Thomas Beecham, and then played Elgar's violin concerto with the ageing composer, propped on a red velvet stool, conducting.

He was appointed director of the Bath Festival in 1959, and served in that capacity for ten years. There were some exhilarating occasions during that period. In 1964 Margot

Hannah More—portrait by H. W. Pickersgill.

Sir Charles Napier—portrait by E. W. Gill.

Horatio Nelson—portrait by W. Beechey.

John Palmer—portrait by G. Dance.

Fonteyn and Rudolf Nureyev danced to Menuhin's playing of a movement from Bartok's Solo Sonata. Two years later, he conducted Mozart's *Cosi Fan Tutte* at the Theatre Royal, with his own orchestra in the pit. In 1968 he staged another Mozart opera, *The Impresario*, but the city authorities declined to underwrite his budget, and he had to rescue the project by what he called 'private donation'. Soon afterwards he resigned, and was succeeded by Michael Tippett. But Bath gave him an exuberant farewell. He had been awarded the Freedom of the city in 1966; and on the last evening of his final Bath festival, he conducted his orchestra in a programme of Strauss waltzes in the candle-lit Assembly Rooms, with the audience dressed in costumes appropriate to the music; they were, he wrote later, 'just as exhilarated as Strauss and I meant them to be'.

During his involvement with the festival, Mr. Menuhin stayed regularly, with his family, at the Lansdown Grove Hotel.

MONTAGU, Elizabeth (1720-1800)
16 Royal Crescent

Because of her penchant for literary *causeries*, and for her dedicated efforts to replace cards with conversation, Mrs. Montagu became known as 'Queen of the Bluestockings'. She was a celebrated hostess in the eighteenth century who gave genteel parties at her London home and at Bath, where the emphasis was on intellectual talk. Conversation, in Mrs. Montagu's view, was infinitely preferable to gambling with cards or dice, which she heartily disliked.

Her husband was Edward Montagu, a wealthy man who was a grandson of the first Earl of Sandwich; they were devoted to each other, but they led individual lives, and

Mrs. Montagu found a great deal of fulfilment in Bath, where she lived in several houses—in Orange Court, Edgar Buildings, Gay Street, Queen's Parade, the Circus and Royal Crescent. She entertained frequently, and Fanny Burney, Mrs. Thrale, Lady Huntingdon, Christopher Anstey and Lord Lyttleton, among others, enjoyed her hospitality, and the conversation that she so assiduously engendered.

The house she occupied in Royal Crescent appears to have been No. 16. She refers to it in one of her letters as 'the centre house', and goes on to say 'the beautiful situation of the Crescent cannot be understood by any comparison with anything in any town whatsoever'.

MORE, Hannah (1745-1833)
76 Great Pulteney Street

Hannah More was a philanthropist and a pioneer of popular education who was known and admired by many notable people in the eighteenth and early nineteenth centuries. She was an intimate friend of David Garrick and his wife, and knew Burke, Dr. Johnson, Reynolds, Mrs. Montagu, Wilberforce and several other famous figures. She wrote novels, plays and poetry, and published a number of moral and religious tracts. The poverty and distress that she witnessed in the Cheddar district of Somerset impelled her to institute Sunday schools there, and an abiding interest in education, shared by her four sisters, dominated her life. The poet Southey wrote: 'Her manners are mild, her information considerable, and her taste correct. There are five sisters, and each of them would be remarked in a mixed company; they pay for, and direct, the education of a thousand poor children . . . '

Miss More lived for ten years, from 1792 to 1802, at No. 76 Great Pulteney Street, and a bronze tablet commemorates her stay there. She died in 1833, leaving £30,000 in legacies to religious societies and charitable institutions.

MORRIS, Jan (1926-   )
9 Marlborough Buildings

Jan Morris is one of the most accomplished travel and historical writers of our day. She worked on the editorial staffs of the *Times* and the *Guardian* before embarking on full-time authorship, and since then has written something like a score of books, the best known of which is probably *Venice,* a perceptive survey of the famous city, originally published in 1960.

She has a great affection for Bath, and lived for a time at No. 9 Marlborough Buildings. In an admirable introduction to Charles Robertson's *Bath: an Architectural Guide,* she has this to say about the city: 'But catch the right day, the right wind, and then Bath can be the very happiest city in England. Then the crescents and squares look no longer regimented, but benign and comradely. Then the grey deserts the stone, and the gold creeps back. The average age of the populace seems to drop by twenty years or so, the tables outside the pubs are full and lively, long skirts swish down Milsom Street, guitar music sounds from the upstairs pads of Park Street. Bath seems full of flowers then, and the little pedestrian alleys in the city centre are bright with fruit, trendy clothes and *Private Eye,* and on the green below the Royal Crescent the small boys of the Jamaican community set up their stumps and play deft and hilarious cricket in the sun'.

Jan Morris has now left Bath for the remoter charms of Wales, where she continues to write. Her love of Venice inspired a second book on the city, *The Venetian Empire*, which was published in 1980.

NAPIER, Sir Charles James (1782-1853)
10 Henrietta Street

During the second half of the eighteenth century George Napier, an army colonel who had served in America, fathered a remarkable quartette of sons. Three of them had outstanding careers in the army, serving with Sir John Moore in Spain and Portugal in 1808-09; ultimately all three were knighted and became generals. Another son, the youngest, achieved the rank of captain in the navy, wrote an authoritative history of Florence, and was elected a Fellow of the Royal Society.

Sir Charles James Napier was the eldest of the three military prodigies. As a major-general he was sent to India in 1841, to take command of the province of Sind, which was on the brink of war; with a force of 2,800, he defeated an army of 22,000 tribesmen, and restored peace to the region, earning the warm congratulations of Wellington, and becoming known as 'the Conqueror of Sind'. He lived in Bath in 1838-40, just before he went out to India. His house was No. 10 Henrietta Street, and a bronze tablet records his tenancy there.

NAPIER, Sir William Francis Patrick (1785-1860)
19 Green Park

In 1841, when Sir Charles Napier was posted to India his brother, William Napier, took up residence at No. 19 Green Park. He had retired from the army on half-pay in 1819, and for several years he had been collecting material for his *History of the War in the Peninsular.* The book, long and authoritative, was published between 1828 and 1840, and translated into French, Spanish, Italian, German and Persian; it established Napier permanently as a major historical writer. He became a major-general in 1841, and then served for five years as lieutenant-governor of Guernsey. Other books followed, including *The Conquest of Scinde* (1844-46), a defence of his brother's campaign in India, and a biography of Sir Charles Napier. He was awarded the KCB in 1848, and was promoted general in 1859, the year before his death.

NAPOLEON III, Louis Napoleon Bonaparte (1808-1873)
*55 Great Pulteney Street

Louis Napoleon Bonaparte was a nephew of the great Napoleon, and was Emperor of France from 1852 until 1871, at the time of the Second Empire. The end of his reign occurred after the Franco-Prussian war (1870-71), in which he was captured by the Germans at Sedan, and held prisoner for the duration. Soon afterwards he was deposed by the National Assembly, and retired to England with his wife and family.

He came to Bath on several occasions. The first time was

69

in 1846, when he stayed for six weeks at the Sydney Hotel (now the Holburne of Menstrie Museum) at the top of Great Pulteney Street; Walter Savage Landor, who was then living at No. 35 St. James's Square, dined with him every day during this visit. After he was deposed in 1871, and during the last two years of his life, he often stayed at No. 55 Great Pulteney Street, where a bronze tablet records his occupancy.

NASH, Richard, Beau Nash (1674-1761)
Sawclose; St. John's Court

Three men are generally considered to have been responsible for Bath's emergence as a fashionable resort in the early part of the eighteenth century; they were Ralph Allen, the philanthropist, John Wood senior, the architect, and Beau Nash, the extrovert impresario who dominated the life of the city for nearly half a century. Nash's contribution is principally a social one. G. M. Trevelyan remarks, in his *English Social History,* that 'during his long supremacy as Master of the Ceremonies, nearly covering the reigns of Anne and the first two Georges, Nash did perhaps as much as any other person, even in the eighteenth century, to civilise the neglected manners of mankind'. The strict code of conduct that he drew up for those attending social events in Bath became widely accepted, and was chiefly responsible for a marked improvement in general behaviour. At Bath functions, for example, gentlemen were not allowed to wear riding boots or swords, and duelling was banned; members of the aristocracy were firmly told that rudeness to fellow guests of lower station would not be tolerated; and ladies were informed that their apparel and behaviour should be beyond reproach: his rule in this later context was unequivocal—'Ladies dressing and behaving like Handmaids must not be surprised if they are treated like Handmaids'.

Nash came to Bath in 1705, after half-heartedly pursuing careers in the army and as a lawyer. The gambling craze that gripped the city undoubtedly attracted him; but within a short time of his arrival he was appointed Master of the Ceremonies, with virtual control over all Bath's social life. His skill and good fortune at gambling brought him prosperity, and he was able to live in a fine mansion in St. John's Court, now the 'Garrick's Head' public house. In 1739, however, an act was passed making several popular card games illegal, and Nash's income declined drastically. So did his reputation; in 1743, when he was seventy, he was described as 'a silly overlord, a wornout and toothless old man crowned with a white hat, and whose face was animated iron rust, changeless and shameless red'. He was obliged to leave St. John's Court, and take a smaller house in the Sawclose. Here he lived with his mistress, a dressmaker called Juliana Papjoy; and when he was accused of being a whoremonger, he proved that his reputation as a wit was unsullied by age. 'A man can no more be termed a whoremonger for having one whore in his house' he replied, 'than a cheesemonger for having one cheese'. He died in February 1761, at the age of eighty-seven, and was given a magnificent civic funeral, and buried at the Abbey. In the Pump Room today, his statue by Prince Hoare gazes down at visitors with obvious disapproval, from an alcove at the east end of the room.

His last house, close to the Theatre Royal's entrance, is now a restaurant called 'Popjoy's'. The slight discrepancy in the name is not accidental. Nash's mistress was officially Juliana Popjoy; but her relationship with the Beau was almost certainly responsible, at the time, for the coarse adaptation, 'Papjoy', by which she became generally known.

A bronze tablet on the house commemorates Nash's tenancy there.

NELSON, Horatio, 1st Viscount Nelson (1758-1805)
2 Pierrepont Street

The great sailor is believed to have first visited Bath in 1772, accompanying his father, the Rector of Burnham Thorpe in Norfolk, who came regularly to the city to take the waters. Nelson was a fourteen-year-old midshipman at the time, newly enlisted in the navy, and Gainsborough painted his portrait, showing him in a smart blue uniform, standing at a table with an open book on navigation before him. Gainsborough was then living at No. 17 The Circus, and the painting was probably completed there.

Nine years later, when he was twenty-two and already a Post-Captain, Nelson returned to Bath for a lengthier stay. His health had been badly impaired after thirty months' continuous service in the Caribbean, culminating in the ill-fated expedition to San Juan; and when he was granted extensive leave to convalesce, he decided that Bath was the place in which his recovery would best be expedited. He arrived in the autumn of 1780, and took lodgings at No. 2 Pierrepont Street, the home of an apothecary called Spry. A full course of 'physic', prescribed by Dr. Woodward of Gay Street, together with the much-vaunted therapy of the waters and the baths, slowly restored his strength; and late in 1781 he was able to write to his great friend Captain Locker: 'My health, I thank God, is perfectly restored, although I shall remain here a few weeks longer, that it may be firmly fixed, as also to avoid the cold weather which I believe is setting in—for, you know, this is like Jamaica to any other part of England'.

He returned to Bath again in September 1797, to stay with his wife and father, after losing an arm in Teneriffe. His previous visits to the city had been as a midshipman and a Post-Captain. Now he was Rear-Admiral Sir Horatio Nelson, and Bath, having awarded him the Freedom of the city after the great naval victory of Cape St. Vincent, acclaimed him as a hero. One of the local journals was euphoric: 'Arrived at Bath . . . Admiral Sir Horatio Nelson . . . The Rear-Admiral, who was received at Portsmouth on the 1st with a universal greeting, reached Bath on Sunday evening in good health and spirits, to the great joy of his Lady and Venerable Father, and gratification of every admirer of British Valour . . .' He remained in the city for a fortnight, and the wound occasioned by the amputation of his right arm at Santa Cruz in Teneriffe was dressed daily by a surgeon; then in mid-September, he travelled to London with his wife, breaking the journey at Newbury *en route*.

Nelson's father spent a great deal of time in Bath, and died at his lodgings in Pulteney Street three years before his famous son was killed at Trafalgar in 1805. Lady Nelson, too, visited the city frequently. In 1809 she was staying at No. 2 Bennett Street; and at the same time, another lady highly esteemed by the late Admiral was enjoying the ambience of Bath at No. 6 Edward Street, not very far away. But Emma Hamilton's extravagancies and gambling excesses were rapidly reducing her to penury, and the generous legacies left her by her husband and Nelson had already been squandered. She was to spend twelve months in a debtors' prison in 1813, and to die in abject poverty two years later.

The house in Pierrepont Street carries a bronze plaque unveiled in 1904 by Lord Selbourne, First Lord of the Admiralty. A decade ago it was empty, and its dirty windows and rusting paintwork drew protests from several citizens. Now it provides accommodation for a secretarial college, and its appearance has been modestly improved.

Other evidences of Nelson's assocations with Bath are to be seen at the western end of New King Street. Nelson Place and Nile Street were named in his honour after the great victory of the Nile in 1798. So, too, was Norfolk Crescent—so called because Norfolk was the Admiral's home county.

NOBLE, Lady Celia (1870-1962)
22 Royal Crescent

Lady Celia Noble lived at No. 22 Royal Crescent for many years, and died there in 1962 at the age of ninety-two. She was a grand-daughter of Isambard Kingdom Brunel, the celebrated engineer who built the Great Western Railway and designed the revolutionary steamship *Great Eastern.* Her father, Arthur James, was an assistant master at Eton, and her mother was Brunel's daughter, Florence. After her marriage to Saxton Noble, who later succeeded to a baronetcy, she became well known as a hostess in musical and artistic circles in London, and after she came to Bath she continued, for many years, to arrange concerts of chamber music at her home in the Crescent. Princess Marie-Louise, a grand-daughter of Queen Victoria, stayed with her whenever she came to Bath, and Queen Mary, consort of George V, visited her frequently during the last war. Her salon was the last of a line that stretched back to Mrs. Montagu in the eighteenth century.

OLIVER, William, MD (1695-1764)
*Queen Square, west side

When Queen Square was completed by John Wood the Elder in 1734, its west side consisted of three separate houses. The centre house, standing back from its two neighbours, was occupied by William Oliver, probably the most celebrated of Bath's long succession of doctors. With Ralph Allen, Beau Nash and the elder Wood, he played an important part in the creation of the Mineral Water Hospital; he was its chief physician at its inception in 1740, and served in that capacity for twenty-one years. Perhaps his greatest claim to fame is as the inventor of the Bath Oliver biscuit, which he prescribed for patients undergoing a special diet while taking a course of the waters; it is still made to his recipe, and is enjoyed all over the world.

In 1830 Oliver's house in Queen Square was demolished, and its two flanking buildings were joined by a neo-classical structure that now houses the Reference Library. A bronze tablet on the façade carries the following legend: 'On this site stood the residence of William Oliver, MD, one of the founders of the Royal Mineral Water Hospital. 1695-1764'.

OLIVIER, Laurence, Lord Olivier (1907-   )
Royal Crescent Hotel

Lord Olivier's towering status as an actor has been built up over a period of more than fifty years. He established his reputation in 1931 in *Private Lives,* with Noel Coward and Gertrude Lawrence, and during his long assocation with the Old Vic company, he became celebrated for his Shakespearean roles. He produced and directed three films,

Henry V, Hamlet and *Richard III,* in which he starred; and throughout a long, active life, his outstanding contributions to the theatre and the cinema have won him countless admirers throughout the world. He came to Bath in 1980, when his wife, Joan Plowright, played in *Filumena* at the Theatre Royal. Lord and Lady Olivier stayed at the Royal Crescent Hotel on that occasion.

PALMER, John (1742-1818)
1 North Parade Buildings

Some time during 1772, the following announcement appeared in the *Morning Post:* 'The Bath mail did not arrive so soon by several hours on Monday, owing to the mailman getting a little intoxicated on his way between Newbury and Marlborough, and falling from his horse into a hedge, where he was found asleep by means of his dog'. At that time the mails were carried in relays by mounted post-boys, and the kind of incident recorded above was far from uncommon. John Palmer suggested that mail should be carried in stage-coaches—a fairly obvious solution, it would seem, although the Post Office had rejected it as impracticable. But Palmer persisted and, in 1784, the first mail-coach ran from London to Bristol. By the following year the innovation was firmly established, and revenue from the mails increased appreciably. Palmer was made Comptroller-General of the Post Office, but was obliged to retire on pension after a quarrel with the Postmaster-General; he was eventually awarded £50,000 as compensation for the loss of his job—a handsome golden handshake indeed, and one that caused a great deal of controversy.

Palmer was born in Bath, and was the son of the proprietor of the Bath and Bristol theatres. After his retirement from the Post Office, eighteen towns, including Bath, presented him with their Freedom. He was twice Mayor of Bath, and four times MP for the city. Like Ralph Allen before him, his Post Office reforms made him a very wealthy man.

His home was at No. 1 North Parade Buildings, and the bronze tablet there was unveiled in April 1901, by the Marquis of Londonderry, then Postmaster-General.

PARRY, Dr. Caleb Hillier (1755-1822)
27 the Circus

Dr. Caleb Hillier Parry came to Bath in 1779, a year after obtaining his MD at Edinburgh; he probably realised the potential for success that awaited a well-qualified medical practitioner in a city that catered extensively for the sick and infirm. He lived first at No. 13 Catharine Place, and later moved to No. 27 the Circus, where a bronze tablet records his tenancy. He became physician to the Bath General Hospital, later to be known as the Royal Mineral Water Hospital.

He practised in Bath when the city was at the peak of its fame and popularity, and he prospered accordingly. At the outset, his practice afforded him £40 a year; before his retirement, he was earning £3,000 a year. One day, when he was well established a friend, talking to him in the street, commented on the way his large waistcoat pockets bulged. 'I suppose there are guineas in there?' he suggested mildly. Parry agreed. 'Yes', he replied, 'I believe there are ninety-nine, and I may make it a round sum before I get home'.

His medical researches were of considerable importance, and a monograph that he published in 1816 on *The Nature, Cause and Varieties of the Arterial Pulse* was widely praised in medical circles. His collection of nine hundred books on medicine was moved to Bristol University in 1949-50, and now forms part of the medical library there. He was the father of Sir William Edward Parry, the Arctic explorer.

PARRY, Sir William Edward (1790-1865)
27 the Circus

Between 1819 and 1825 William Edward Parry, as a young naval commander, undertook three voyages of exploration to the Arctic, in an attempt to discover the North-west Passage. In the wooden sailing ships of the time, the expeditions were hazardous in the extreme; but he effected a passage through Lancaster Sound into the Arctic Ocean, and Parry Island, in that desolate area, has been named after him. On his return, he was justifiably hailed as a hero. Later, in 1827, he tried to reach the North Pole from Spitzbergen, travelling across the ice with sledges, but the southwards drift of the floes finally defeated him.

He became hydrographer to the Admiralty, was given a knighthood in 1829, and later promoted rear-admiral. Bath awarded him the Freedom of the city in recognition of his outstanding contribution to the progress of Arctic exploration.

Parry lived at No. 27 the Circus during his boyhood and youth. His father, Caleb Hillier Parry, was a doctor who practised there for many years; and a bronze tablet on the house celebrates the achievements of both men.

PEPYS, Samuel (1633-1703)
The Bear Inn (possibly)

The famous diary of Samuel Pepys, written in cipher, remained in Magdalene College, Cambridge, for more than a hundred years before it was first published in 1825. It is a completely fascinating document of more than a million and a quarter words, covering the years from 1660 to 1669; and as Arthur Bryant has said, 'after three centuries, there is not a page in it that does not arrest the reader, and quicken his perception of humanity'.

In the diary Pepys describes his visit to 'the Bath' as he called it (the seventeenth-century name usually included the article), on 12th June, 1668. When he arrived, he found 'the town most of stone and clean, though the streets generally narrow'. On the morning after his arrival he rose at 4 a.m. and went to the Cross Bath, where he stayed in the steaming water for two hours. He was mildly shocked at the number of 'fine ladies' bathing, and thought that 'it cannot be clean to go so many bodies together in the same water'. Then, 'wrap in a sheet', he was carried to his lodgings in a chair, and went to bed, 'sweating for an hour'. He paid the sergeant of the bath ten shillings for the privilege of immersing himself, and the man who carried him in a chair was given three shillings and sixpence—generous rates indeed, when one considers the disparities in money values over three hundred years.

It is not known where Pepys stayed when he came to Bath; but he could well have lodged at the old Bear Inn, which was demolished in 1806 to make way for Union Street.

PHILLIP, Vice-Admiral Arthur (1738-1814)
19 Bennett Street

Admiral Phillip was one of Britain's early empire-builders. After long service in the Royal Navy, he was sent to Australia in 1787 to establish a penal colony there, in what is now New South Wales. He was selected for the task by the Home Secretary, Viscount Sydney; and after founding a settlement on the harbour of Port Jackson, he named it Sydney, after the man who had sent him there.

Phillip remained in Australia for six years, and became the first governor of New South Wales. Under his control the colony prospered, and peace was established with the aboriginal natives. He wrote to Viscount Sydney: 'This country will prove the most valuable acquisition Great Britain has ever made'. Today his statue, a monument to his pioneering efforts, overlooks Sydney Harbour.

He returned to England in 1793 and retired to Bath, taking a house at No. 19 Bennett Street. His health, however, was far from robust, and towards the end of his life a stroke deprived him of the use of his right arm and leg; he could occasionally be seen circumnavigating the Circus in a Bath chair. He died in 1814, the year before Waterloo.

PICKWICK, Moses (1782-1869)
8 Henrietta Street; 7 Laura Place

There is little doubt that Dickens encountered the name Pickwick on one of his first visits to Bath—probably in 1835, when he visited the city as a parliamentary reporter, to cover a speech by Lord John Russell for the *Morning Chronicle*. At that time Moses Pickwick was the landlord of

Samuel Pepys—portrait by J. Hayls.

Sir Isaac Pitman—portrait by Sir A. S. Cope.

William Pitt—portrait by J. Hoppner.

Alexander Pope—portrait by W. Hoare.

the *White Hart,* one of Bath's oldest and most famous inns: it appears on Gilmore's map of the city published in 1694, and was demolished in 1867. Pickwick was an enterprising fellow who operated the coach service between London and Bath, and his name was prominently painted on the doors of all his vehicles. His great-grandfather, Eleazer Pickwick, had been a foundling, saved by some compassionate soul in the village of Pickwick, and given the name of the place where he had been found.

Moses Pickwick prospered handsomely from his stewardship of the 'White Hart', and from his control of the Bath to London coach service. Few details are available about him, and the address of his home in Bath is indeterminate; he is said to have lived, after his retirement from the *White Hart,* at No. 8 Henrietta Street, and No. 7 Laura Place. At the height of his career as a landlord and a coach proprietor, he is believed to have owned a string of three hundred horses.

His was not the only name that Bath provided for *Pickwick Papers.* When Dickens visited the city in 1835, the landlord of a hostelry in Trim Street called the *Caledonian Inn,* was a gentleman with the illustrious name of Alexander Snodgrass. The novelist substituted 'Augustus' for 'Alexander', and immortalised him as a poetic member of the Pickwick Club.

PITMAN, Sir Isaac (1813-1897)
17 Royal Crescent

The invention of shorthand is usually credited to Sir Isaac Pitman, although Samuel Taylor had published *An Essay intended to establish . . . an universal system of Stenography* as early as 1786. Pitman adapted Taylor's principle, and produced a much more practical and sophisticated method. He invented a system of phonography, or writing by sound, in 1837, and finally produced the famous shorthand system that is always linked with his name.

As a young man, he was dismissed from his job as a schoolmaster at Wotton-under-Edge in Gloucestershire, because he joined the 'New Church' founded by Emmanuel Swedenborg. Soon afterwards, in 1839, he came to Bath, and lived at No. 5 Nelson Place for four years. He loved the city, and at that time he wrote : 'Of the many beautiful cities in this fair country, Bath is unquestionably the most beautiful'. Much later in his life he took a house in the Royal Crescent (No. 12), and seven years later, in 1896, he moved to No. 17, where a bronze tablet commemorates his tenancy. He died there, at the age of eighty-four, on 22nd January, 1897.

Throughout his long life he was a man of regular habits and unshakeable convictions. A London newspaper described him as 'teetotaller, vegetarian, Swedenborgian, anti-vaccinationist, non-smoker, spelling reformer, and inventor of phonography. At 84 he was still working hard at his desk at 6.30 every morning, summer and winter'. And there can be no doubt that his rigorous self-discipline brought him happiness and fulfilment; the day before he died, he wrote a brief note to the Rev. Gordon Drummond, Minister of the New Church at Bath, in which he said 'To those who ask how Isaac Pitman died, say, Peacefully, and with no more concern than in passing from one room to another, to take up some further employment.'

PITT, William, the Elder, Lord Chatham
(1708-1778)
*7 the Circus

The great statesman was a martyr to gout throughout his life; he even suffered as a boy of sixteen when he was at Eton. Although his many visits to Bath were primarily occasioned by the affliction, he served as its MP from 1757 to 1766, and was awarded the Freedom of the city in 1757. Two years earlier, he had bought a house at No. 7 the Circus, which he maintained for ten years. The bronze tablet over the door was unveiled by Lord Rosebery, the great Liberal statesman, in 1902.

Although Pitt was an outstanding administrator, a compelling parliamentary orator, and a successful Foreign Minister during the Seven Years War against France, he had an unstable temperament that was undoubtedly caused by the illness, both mental and physical, that plagued him throughout his life. But he was a great patriot. 'He loved England', said Macaulay, 'as an Athenian loved the city of the violet crown, as a Roman loved the city of the seven hills'. And for a brilliant impression of him at Bath, we need look no further than Thackeray's delightful cameo in his *Lectures on the Four Georges:* 'And if you and I had been alive then, and strolling down Milsom Street—hush! We should have taken our hats off, as an awful long, lean figure, swathed in flannels, passed by in its chair, and a livid face looked out from the window—great fierce eyes staring from under a bushy, powdered wig, a terrible frown, a terrible Roman nose—and we whisper "There he is! There's the great commoner! There is Mr. Pitt!" '.

PITT, William, the Younger (1759-1806)
15 Johnstone Street

'He is not a chip of the old block', said Burke, referring to Lord Chatham's second son, 'he is the old block himself'. In fact, the younger Pitt's career was even more illustrious than that of his father. He was Chancellor of the Exchequer when he was twenty-three, and Prime Minister of Great Britain before he was twenty-five—from 1783 until 1801, and again from 1804 until his death in 1806. In 1784 he was invited to stand as MP for Bath, but was defeated; later in the same year he was awarded the Freedom of the city, an honour that had been bestowed on his father twenty-seven years previously.

He lived at No. 15 Johnstone Street in 1802, and a bronze tablet on the house, unveiled by Lord Rosebery in 1902, celebrates the fact. In 1806, during another visit to Bath, he called at Shockerwick House, the home of John Wiltshire, just outside the city. Wiltshire's father had operated a prosperous carrier service between Bath and the 'White Swan' at Holborn Bridge, London, and had transported many of Gainsborough's canvases to the capital for framing; and as a mark of his gratitude, the artist had bequeathed him several of his paintings, including a widely praised portrait of the parish clerk of Bradford-on-Avon. It was to see these paintings that Pitt had gone to Shockerwick. But while he was there, a messenger arrived at the house with the news of Napoleon's crushing victory over Britain's allies at Austerlitz. Pitt was so distressed by the news that he fainted; and his health was so seriously impaired by the shock that he died two weeks later.

POPE, Alexander (1688-1744)
Prior Park

When Pope visited Bath for the first time in 1714, he praised the city in a letter to a friend, declaring that it had 'the finest promenades in the world'. Afterwards, he came regularly during the season, and often stayed with Ralph Allen at Prior Park.

The two men became close friends. Later, however, they quarrelled; and in his will Pope compounded the breach by leaving Allen a legacy of £150, 'being to the best of my calculations, the amount of what I have received from him'. It was an ungracious gesture, and Allen immediately handed the bequest to a charity.

Pope was physically a tiny man; he was only four feet six inches tall, and an attack of tuberculosis when he was a child had left him with permanent curvature of the spine. His poetry, however, was seldom marred by his physical disabilities, and some of the splendid epigrams in his *Essay on Criticism* are still widely quoted today; 'To err is human, to forgive divine' and 'Fools rush in where angels fear to tread' are just two of his polished phrases that can be said to have passed into the English language.

QUIN, James (1693-1766)
*3 Pierrepont Street

James Quin, actor and wit, spent the last fifteen years of his life in retirement at Bath, lodging in the house of Mrs. Simpson at No. 3 Pierrepont Street. He was a bluff, genial character in the mould of Falstaff, a part he played frequently at Drury Lane and Covent Garden; and during his retirement, he was friendly with many of the famous people who stayed at Bath. He often dined at Ralph Allen's splendid house at Prior Park, and on most Friday evenings he was to be found enjoying a lavish meal at the 'Three Tuns', a coaching house in Stall Street. On one occasion he demolished no fewer than six bottles of claret with his dinner; and after being carried home by friends, he gave them instructions that he was not to be disturbed until noon on the following Sunday.

Just before he left London for Bath he quarrelled violently with his manager, an impresario named Rich; afterwards, feeling some contrition for his part in the quarrel, he wrote a very brief note, hoping for a reconciliation. It read: 'Am in Bath—Quin'. The reply was equally brief, and much less friendly. 'Stay there and be damned—Rich' it said. And there, presumably, the relationship ended.

Quin loved Bath, often referring to the city as 'a fine slope to the grave', and saying that he 'did not know a better place for an old cock to roost in'. But he could be sharp with those who tried his patience. A young aspiring actor once asked for an opportunity to recite a Shakespearean soliloquy to him, and when the request was granted began: 'To be or not to be—that is the question'. Quin silenced him with an imperious wave of the hand, and growled 'No question at all, Sir—not to be, upon my honour!'

There is a memorial tablet to him in Bath Abbey, with an epitaph written by David Garrick.

RAUZZINI, Venanzio (1746-1810)
17 Queen Square; 13 Gay Street, Perrymead Villa, Lyncombe.

He came to Bath in 1777 to assist Lamotte, the resident impresario, with the management of concerts at the New

Assembly Rooms. His background was impressive; born in Rome, he had established a wide reputation in Europe as an opera singer and a composer of marked ability. When Lamotte left Bath in 1780, he immediately became director of the Assembly Rooms concerts.

Rauzzini lived at No. 17 Queen Square, and 13 Gay Street, and had another house, Perrymead Villa, at Lyncombe; Haydn visited him there in August, 1794. The Italian singer and composer was held in the highest esteem in Bath, and was buried in the Abbey with some ceremony when he died in 1810. His reputation as a musician has perhaps declined with the years; when Thomas Sturge Cotterell, who conceived the idea of placing bronze tablets on the houses of the famous, was asked why the Italian impresario was not similarly commemorated, he replied, 'While Rauzzini was "on the list" of celebrities to be honoured with a bronze tablet, his name was subsequently removed to the "doubtfuls", the point being the insufficiency of his claims upon posterity's recognition'.

Rauzzini was an outstanding upholder of Bath's long musical tradition. Before the last war, it was the city's proud boast that its Pump Room orchestra was the oldest in Britain, having played continuously every season since 1704. Among the guest performers during the last century were Liszt, the elder Johann Strauss and Sir Arthur Sullivan; and in 1848 Sir Charles Hallé was invited to become musical director. He elected to go to Manchester, and the possibility that a Hallé Orchestra of Bath might have emerged had he chosen otherwise, can only be pondered.

In 1920 the director was a popular musician called Jan Hurst, who enjoyed performing César Franck's Symphony No. 1. On the first occasion it was played, an elderly lady dropped dead in the Pump Room. Another performance was marred when the orchestra's 'cellist stumbled while climbing on to the platform, and broke a leg; and when the symphony was performed for the third time, someone drowned in the baths. It was never played again during Mr. Hurst's term of office.

RICHARDSON, Sir Ralph (1902-   )
Royal Crescent Hotel

Among twentieth-century actors, there are few more illustrious names than Sir Ralph Richardson. He made his first stage appearance at Brighton in 1921, and since then he has undertaken most of the major dramatic roles in the English theatre. He has been president of the National Youth Theatre since 1959. In 1981 he came to Bath to play in David Storey's *Early Days* at the Theatre Royal. During his sojourn in the city, he stayed at the Royal Crescent Hotel.

ROBERTS, Frederick, Field-Marshal Earl Roberts (1832-1914)
*9 Queen's Parade

Between 1900 and 1914 Field-Marshal Lord Roberts stayed frequently at No. 9 Queen's Parade, the home of his sister, Mrs. Sherston. His long and distinguished career as a soldier had reached its peak in 1900, following his success as commander in the Boer War, and he was a much revered figure.

He joined the Bengal Artillery when he was nineteen, served in the Indian Mutiny, and won the VC in 1858, when he was twenty-six. Later he became commander-in-chief in India, and was promoted field-marshal. His appointment to the supreme command in South Africa at the end of 1899 resulted in a rapid improvement in the British conduct of the war, and he was awarded an earldom for his services in saving what had been an extremely difficult situation. He died at St. Omer in France in 1914, when he was on his way to visit the Indian expeditionary force there, of which he was colonel-in-chief.

Lord Roberts stayed at No. 9 Queen's Parade in September, 1902, when the Freedom of the city was presented to him. After the ceremony, he unveiled the tablet on Lord Clive's house at No. 14 the Circus.

His own tablet reads: 'Field-Marshal Earl Roberts KG was a frequent visitor to this house, 1900-1914. Born 1832. Died 1914'. It was unveiled by his daughter, Lady Edwina Lewin.

SAGE, Fanny (c.1762-1835)
20 Royal Crescent

In 1778 a young woman called Fanny Sage came to stay in Bath with her uncle, the Rev. Thomas Sedgwick Whalley, DD. Dr. Whalley lived at No. 20 Royal Crescent; and when he heard that his sister, Mrs. Sage, had died, he immediately offered her daughter the hospitality of his comfortable home.

Fanny stayed at No. 20 for something like ten years. She was an attractive young woman who sang well and played the harpsichord expertly. Romney painted a full-length portrait of her. She became well-known in the city, and her charm and personality, allied to her beauty, earned her the unofficial title of 'Queen of Bath'.

Later Fanny married, and spent most of her time abroad. In 1828 she was widowed, and living in France at La Flèche on the Loire. Her remaining years were spent in complete obscurity recollecting, perhaps, those halcyon days in Bath when she was the toast of the city.

SAINTSBURY, George (1845-1933)
1A Royal Crescent

Adjoining the east end of the Royal Crescent is a small, two-storeyed building that is dwarfed by the bulk of the Crescent's first house. It is numbered 1A, and between 1916 and 1933 it was the home of George Saintsbury, a retired professor of English literature at the University of Edinburgh, and a scholar and man of letters of immense distinction.

Saintsbury was never a public figure in Bath, but he could often be recognised on his morning walks, carrying a string bag full of books, and strolling slowly along Grand Parade; like Lord Rosebery and Rudyard Kipling, he considered the view across the river and over the valley from there to be outstanding. And on most days his venerable head, crowned by a black skull cap, and fringed with a long white beard, could be seen through the ground floor window of his study, as he pored over a book or a manuscript.

He died in 1933. The *Times* newspaper epitomised his achievement succinctly and admirably: 'Seldom does so ripe and so full a scholar and man leave the world of good books and companionable wine as the veteran George Saintsbury, who has just died in the Augustan peace of the Royal Crescent in Bath'.

SCOTT, Sir Walter (1771-1835)
6 South Parade

The faith of many women in the effectiveness of panaceas is almost legendary. Mary of Modena, the wife of James II, came to Bath hoping that a course of the waters would induce pregnancy; Dr. Johnson's mother made the long tiring journey from Lichfield to London with her son, believing that if Queen Anne touched him, his scrofula would be cured; and Sir Walter Scott's aunt brought the future novelist to Bath when he was a four-year-old fledgling, believing that the waters would help to cure his pronounced limp; an attack of poliomyelitis, when he was only eighteen months old, had left him with lameness in the right leg that proved to be permanent. Only the confidence of Mary of Modena, it seems, was justified.

The famous author of the Waverley novels stayed with his aunt at No. 6 South Parade, now part of Pratt's Hotel, and there is a bronze tablet on the wall to commemorate the fact. Scott saw his first play *As You Like It,* at Bath's Theatre Royal during the visit.

SEMPRINI, Albert (1908-   )
Lymore Gardens, Oldfield Park

The popular pianist who entertained radio, television and theatre audiences during the years following the second world war, was born in Oldfield Park, Bath, in 1908. His father was an Italian who played in the Pump Room orchestra; and when he was eleven, young Semprini was sent to Italy to study music at the Conservatorio Verdi in Milan. While he was there, he achieved a small measure of success in the field of conducting, and had the distinction of appearing as a sub-conductor in several opera houses, including La Scala at Milan.

His British passport was seized by Fascist police when he tried to leave Italy, and it was not renewed until 1948. By now he had turned to light music, and when he returned to England he became widely successful as a popular pianist, appearing frequently on television and radio, as well as on the concert platform. He gave a special recital at the Palace Theatre in Bath in September 1953, presenting a programme that included works by Chopin, Liszt, Albeniz and Schumann.

SHELLEY, Percy Bysshe (1792-1822)
5 Abbey Churchyard

In the summer of 1816 Shelley, with William Godwin and his daughter Mary, accompanied by Claire Claremont, visited Switzerland for several weeks. On their return to England they stayed in Bath, at No. 5 Abbey Churchyard, the residence of William Meyler, who operated a circulating library from the premises. Here Shelley corrected the proofs of the latest cantos of Byron's *Childe Harold*, and Mary Godwin pressed on with her novel, *Frankenstein*—an early 'book of the film', one might say. But on December 15th Shelley learned that his wife Harriet (on whom he had settled an allowance of £200 a year), had been drowned in the Serpentine; and a fortnight later, he married Mary Godwin in London. By this time Claire Claremont was living at No. 12 New Bond Street in Bath; and there, in February 1817, she gave birth to Byron's daughter, Allegra.

Shelley and his wife took a house at Marlow in the early spring of 1817, and he seems not to have visited Bath again.
92

His father, Sir Timothy Shelley, stayed at No. 26 the Circus in 1820; and Mary returned to the city nearly a quarter of a century after her husband's death, occupying rooms at No. 14 Queen Square.

SHERIDAN, Richard Brinsley (1751-1816)
9 New King Street

In 1770 Thomas Sheridan, an Irish actor, came with his family to Bath and set up in business as a teacher of elocution in New King Street. His nineteen-year-old son, Richard, had just left Harrow, and was cherishing ambitions to become a playwright; but he was captivated by the charms of Elizabeth Linley, a beautiful and talented singer, who lived with her family at No. 11 Royal Crescent, and their relationship was to affect his life considerably. In March, 1772, he eloped with her to France from the house in Royal Crescent, and when they returned to England, he fought two duels with a Captain Mathews, a rival for the lady's favours. In the second encounter he was seriously wounded, and several weeks passed before he finally recovered. Sheridan and Miss Linley eventually married and in 1775 his first play, *The Rivals* was produced. He was now the proprietor of the Drury Lane theatre in London, and two years later his great masterpiece, *The School for Scandal,* was staged there.

In 1780 the burgesses of Stafford elected Sheridan as their MP, and he was soon acknowledged as an able parliamentarian and an accomplished orator. He became a close friend of the Prince of Wales, and developed a reputation as a wit. One evening he was seen by a friend in a Covent Garden coffee house, casually pouring wine as he watched his Drury Lane theatre being destroyed by fire.

The friend expressed astonishment at his calm indifference to the disaster, and Sheridan's reply became the talk of the town. 'Surely', he said, 'a man may be allowed to drink a glass of wine by his own fireside!'.

He was always short of money, and regularly lived on credit. 'I've just bought a new house' he told Lord Guildford, 'Now everything will go like clockwork'. 'Ay', said his lordship, 'Tick-tick'. Debts plagued him to the end of his days, and during his last illness, officers were stationed at his house to keep his creditors at bay. When he died in July 1816, his body was smuggled away in a blanket, to avoid body-snatching bailiffs.

In his early days at Bath, Sheridan is believed to have lived close to the present No. 9 New King Street. The house, with its near neighbours, has been demolished to make way for more recent dwellings. On the wall of the new No. 9 is a small plaque with the following inscription:

> 'Near this site between 1770-1772
> lived Thomas Sheridan, actor and orthoepist,
> Richard Brinsley Sheridan, dramatist, 1751-1816.'

SICKERT, Walter Richard (1860-1942)
St. George's Hill, Bathampton

The distinguished British impressionist, a pupil of Whistler and a life-long friend of Degas, visited Bath in the summers of 1916 and 1917, when he painted Pulteney Bridge and Belvedere, as well as other aspects of the city. Bath appealed to him strongly, and later in his life he decided to settle there; just before the last war he took a Georgian house at St. George's Hill, Bathampton, where he spent four peaceful years before his death in January, 1942. He was a patron of the Bath College of Art, and lectured there every Friday morning.

He tended, like many artists, to be unorthodox in dress, and his tongue could be waspish. In the early 1920s he attended a dinner in Chelsea, given by Sir Osbert Sitwell, where the English painter and writer, Wyndham Lewis, was among the guests. After the meal, Sickert gave Lewis a cigar with the words 'I give you this cigar because I so greatly admire your writings' and before Lewis could utter his thanks, he added 'If I liked your paintings I'd give you a bigger one!'

SIDDONS, Sarah (1755-1831)
33 the Paragon

When she made her first appearance at Drury Lane, as Portia in the *Merchant of Venice,* Sarah Siddons was a flop; one critic wrote 'She is certainly very pretty—but then, how awkward, and what a shocking dresser . . .' Three years later, however, when she appeared for the first time at Bath's Theatre Royal in *The School for Scandal,* she was rapturously received. She played in the city for four seasons, achieving her greatest success as Lady Macbeth.

Later, she was invited to join the Drury Lane company in London, and she appeared there in October, 1780, at a salary of £10 per week. She was an immediate success in a play called *The Fatal Marriage;* according to a contemporary, 'men wept, and women fainted, or were caried out in fits of hysterics'. She was hailed by the *Morning Post* as 'the first tragic actress now on the English stage', and for the next thirty years, until her retirement in 1812, her supremacy was unchallenged. Her last performance was at Covent Garden as Lady Macbeth, acknowledged to be by far her greatest role. The packed audience in the theatre insisted that the play should end after her last scene, and she had to be led weeping from the stage.

Henderson, one of the great actors of the day, described Mrs. Siddons as 'an actress who never has had an equal, nor could ever have a superior'. She was beautiful, sensitive and intelligent, and her stage presence was striking; but her temperament could be variable, and there were many of her contemporaries who maintained that she inspired more admiration than affection.

When at Bath at the outset of her career, she stayed at No. 2 Abbey Green. Later, when she was firmly established, she took a house at No. 33 the Paragon, and there she lived happily for several years—engagements permitting—with her husband and children. She died in 1831, and was buried in St. Mary's, Paddington, where five thousand mourners gathered to pay tribute to her. A statue of her, by Chantrey, stands in Westminster Abbey.

The bronze tablet on the house in the Paragon was unveiled by Miss Ellen Terry in October, 1922.

SMITH, Henry Stafford (1843-1903)
13 George Street

In the nineteenth century philately was very much in its infancy; so Henry Stafford Smith was something of a pioneer when he opened a shop at No. 13 George Street, for the sale of foreign postage stamps. It was the first shop of its kind in England, and the bronze tablet on the wall in George Street reminds us of his enterprise. The inscription reads: 'These premises were formerly occupied by the philatelist Henry Stafford Smith (1843-1903) who, with his brother William Smith, published from 1863 onwards, *The Stamp Collector's Magazine.* This was the pioneer philatelic

Richard Brinsley Sheridan—portrait by J. Russell.

Sarah Siddons—portrait by G. Stuart.

Tobias George Smollett—artist unknown.

William Makepeace Thackeray—portrait by S. Laurence.

journal, and Bath is therefore the cradle of philatelic literature.'

SMITH, John Christopher (1712-1795)
18 Brock Street

On one of Handel's several visits to Germany early in the eighteenth century, he is said to have met an Englishman, John Christopher Smith, who was so captivated by the composer's character and genius that he accompanied him back to England, 'where he regulated the expenses of his public performances, and filled the office of treasurer with great fidelity'. In other words, Smith became Handel's manager and secretary. He was a musician in his own right, and composed an opera, *Ulysses* and several oratorios; but principally, he was Handel's amanuensis, and when the great man became blind in 1752, it was Smith who copied his scores, and conducted many performances of his famous oratorios.

Handel was not unappreciative. When he died in 1759, he bequeathed £2,000 to Smith—a considerable amount in those days—as well as all his manuscripts, and his beloved harpsichord. To his great credit, Smith refused an offer of £2,000 for the manuscripts from the King of Prussia; and in gratitude to George III, who had granted him a pension, he ensured that they would stay in England by presenting them to the King. The manuscripts are now in the British Library.

Smith retired in 1774, and came to live in Bath, taking a house at No. 18 Brock Street. He lived there, in reasonable comfort one imagines, until his death in 1795 at the venerable age of eighty-three. The bronze plaque adorning the house was unveiled in October 1954, by Mr. Frank Homes.

SMITH, Admiral Sir Sydney (1764-1840)
12 Catharine Place

Although he was inclined to be theatrical, and to boast unduly of his achievements, Admiral Sir Sydney Smith was brave and resourceful, and his naval career was a distinguished one. He fought at St. Vincent, and although he was later captured by the French off Le Havre, and spent two years in a Paris prison, he managed to escape, and returned to defeat them spectacularly at the siege of Saint Jean d'Acre. He was promoted admiral in 1821, died in Paris nineteen years later, and was buried in the Père Lachaise cemetery there.

He was educated at Bath Grammar School, and lived as a boy at Catharine Place (No. 12) for two years, from 1772 to 1774. His headmaster was the Rev. Nathaniel Morgan who often boasted, in later years that he had 'flogged the man who flogged the French'.

SMITH, William (1769-1839)
29 Great Pulteney Street

In informal academic circles he was known as 'Strata Smith'. In the cloistered confines of the Geological Society in London, he was recognised as the man who founded the science of stratigraphy in Britain. Smith's great contribution was the discovery that various layers of rock contained fossils that characterised each layer—in other words, he related geology to the science of palaeontology.

He published his *Order of the Strata and their Imbedded Organic Remains* in 1799, and then launched himself as a geological engineer in Bath, living at No. 29 Great Pulteney Street, from where he produced several excellent series of maps and a number of important monographs. He stayed in the city for twenty years, but the depression following the Napoleonic Wars affected his business adversely, and he was obliged to move north to Scarborough. The government eventually awarded him a pension of £100 a year, and Dublin University conferred on him a Doctorate of Laws. His place as a pioneer of English geology is firmly established.

SMOLLETT, Tobias (1721-1777)
7 South Parade; Gay Street

Although he was a successful novelist, Smollett cherished an ambition to become an established doctor, and tried to start a practice in Bath. He failed, and his disappointment bred bitterness; and in his last novel, *Humphrey Clinker,* published in 1770, he created a character, a testy old bachelor called Matthew Bramble, who lost no opportunity to pour scorn on the city and its fashionable visitors. *Humphrey Clinker* is written in epistolary form and Bramble, staying in Bath, is given every chance to grumble. He complains about 'the noise, tumult and hurry'; about the sedan chairs standing about in the rain, 'soaking in the open street, till they become so many boxes of wet leather'; and about 'the rage of building . . . contrived without judgement, executed without solidity, and stuck together with so little regard to plan and propriety'.

Smollett's sarcasm was engendered by frustration; had he been able to join the ranks, and share the success, of Bath's fashionable doctors, Matthew Bramble, one feels, would have talked about the city in much more honeyed terms.

Smollett stayed in Bath several times, lodging in Gay Street, No. 7 South Parade and, during his last visit, at the old Bear Hotel, which was eventually demolished to make way for Union Street.

SOUTHEY, Robert (1774-1843)
108 Walcot Street

During the early years of his life Southey stayed in Bath with his rather eccentric maiden aunt, a Miss Tyler, who lived at No. 108 Walcot Street. She was passionately fond of the theatre, and young Southey must have been very familiar with the old Theatre Royal in Orchard Street; he remarked later that he saw more plays before he was seven than after he was twenty.

In the latter part of his life he lived for many years at Greta Hall, Keswick; Coleridge and his family shared the house with him for a time, and with Wordsworth at Grasmere nearby, the trio became known as the Lake Poets. Southey was Poet Laureate from 1813 until his death in 1843. He was successively offered the editorship of the *Times*, a seat in parliament, and a baronetcy, all of which he refused, preferring to remain in Keswick and to continue writing. He was a prolific author; in addition to his poetry, he wrote several prose works, including a history of the Peninsular War, a life of Nelson, a history of Brazil and much more—as well as, surprisingly, a little tale called 'The Three Bears', which was to become a classic fairy story. It can be found in his book *The Doctor*.

THACKERAY, William Makepeace (1811-1863)
17 the Circus

In January 1857, Thackeray arrived in Bath to give his celebrated lectures on *The Four Georges.* He had already visited America to deliver these fascinating reviews of manners and morals in England during the reigns of the Hanoverian kings, and had been rapturously received. The large audiences that crowded into the Banqueting Hall of the Guildhall in Bath were equally enthusiastic; a contemporary scribe, writing in the *Bath Rambler,* declared: 'In exposing so fully and completely the gross animalism of these times, he has performed an important work'. The *Bath Chronicle* was a little more restrained. 'Thackeray's manner is unimpassioned and calm', its reporter wrote, 'but it is impossible to describe the impression which he produces . . . Whatever differences of opinion may be entertained on the subject of Mr. Thackeray's views of the four Georges and their times, there can be no question in any quarter as to the force, felicity and high interest of his lectures'.

The talks were later produced in book form, and they can still be read with absorbing interest; they are a masterly assessment of one of the most eventful periods in British history. Whilst he was in Bath, the novelist stayed with his aunt in Gainsborough's old house at No. 17 the Circus.

THICKNESSE, Philip (1719-1792)
9 Royal Crescent

He was a soldier of fortune, an irascible eccentric and, if he himself is to be believed, the man who persuaded Gainsborough to come to Bath. Ill-tempered and

101

aggressive, with an inordinate capacity for making enemies, he longed for wealth and recognition, and was prepared to follow almost any path that would lead him to either.

Thicknesse settled in Bath in 1749. During his second marriage he lived in East Anglia, where he had purchased the governorship of the Landguard Fort at Harwich. He met Gainsborough in Ipswich, and claims to have convinced the struggling young painter that he could improve his prospects considerably by going to Bath. The advice was sound, and Gainsborough took it; he arrived in the city in 1759, and soon achieved great success as a portrait painter.

Accompanied by his third wife, Thicknesse returned to Bath in 1768, and bought a house at No. 9 Royal Crescent. Six years later, he quarrelled with Gainsborough, and after the artist had left Bath for London, he moved to a cottage behind Lansdown Place called St. Catherine's Hermitage. He wrote extensively at this time, still quarrelled regularly, and travelled in Europe whenever he could. Among his literary effusions were three volumes of revealing memoirs, and *The New Prose Bath Guide,* a factual description of the city which he hoped might rival Anstey's best-seller in popularity. It was not a great success; but it bears the unmistakable stamp of his eccentricity, and can still be read with enjoyment today.

THIRLWALL, Connop, Bishop of St. David's (1797-1875)
59 Great Pulteney Street

Connop Thirlwall was a scholar, a barrister and, during the latter part of his life, a distinguished ecclesiastic. He took holy orders in 1827 when he was thirty, and became a tutor and lecturer before completing his exhaustive *History*

of Greece, on which he worked for almost ten years. Lord
Melbourne made him Bishop of St. David's in 1840, and
with characteristic thoroughness he learned to preach in
Welsh, and travelled extensively throughout his large
diocese.

He came to Bath in the closing years of his life, and lived
at No. 59 Great Pulteney Street, where a bronze tablet
records his tenancy. He died in 1875, and was buried in
Westminster Abbey.

THORNEYCROFT, Peter, Lord Thorneycroft
(1909-   )
Francis Hotel

Like Sheridan before him, Peter Thorneycroft was MP for
Stafford; that was before and during the last war. In post-
war Conservative governments he has served as Minister of
Defence (1962-64) and as Chancellor of the Exchequer
(1957), and for some years was chairman of the Conservative
party. He is an accomplished painter, and is a member of the
Royal Society of British Artists; in 1961 his work was
exhibited at the Trafford Gallery in London. He comes to
Bath occasionally to indulge his hobby, and usually stays at
the Francis Hotel in Queen Square.

THRALE, Mrs. Hester (later Mrs. Piozzi)
(1741-1821)
8 Gay Street; 14 South Parade

She began life as Hester Salusbury, married a rich

Southwark brewer, Henry Thrale, and bore him twelve children before she was thirty-seven. Dr. Johnson, who became her very close friend, disliked Mr. Thrale; his conversation, the Doctor said 'does not show the minute hand, but strikes the hour very correctly'. When Thrale died in 1781, there were many who expected Hester to wed Dr. Johnson; but she surprised society by marrying Gabriel Piozzi, her daughters' singing teacher. They lived in Italy for a time, and after his death she came to Bath in 1814, taking the ornate little house at No. 8 Gay Street; it had been designed by John Wood the Elder for Robert Gay, a London surgeon who owned the land and gave the street its name. But the bronze tablet on its façade commemorates Mrs. Piozzi's tenancy.

She was a small vivacious woman, and a great talker. As an elderly lady in Bath, she was regarded as rather shocking, and someone described her as being 'in a permanent state of rampant senility'. On her eightieth birthday in 1820, she arranged an elaborately spectacular ball in the Lower Rooms, and led off the dancing in sprightly fashion with her nephew, Sir John Salusbury. Eighteen months later she died 'in state', at Clifton in Bristol.

She had visited Bath much earlier, when she was married to Mr. Thrale, In 1776 they lodged at North Parade, and Dr. Johnson called on her there, during his visit to the city in that year. Later, in 1780, Hester and her husband stayed at No. 14 South Parade, where they entertained Fanny Burney and many other celebrities.

VICTORIA, Queen (1819-1901)
Royal York Hotel

Queen Victoria came to Bath in October, 1830; at that time she was the eleven-year-old Princess Victoria, and seven years were to elapse before she succeeded to the throne. She was accompanied by her mother, the Duchess of Kent, and the purpose of the visit was to open the new Victoria Park, named in her honour. The royal party spent two days in the city, staying at the Royal York Hotel, then called York House; and the Princess was able to visit the Assembly Rooms, the Pump Room, Great Pulteney Street, Royal Crescent, and William Beckford's tower at Lansdown.

The room at the Royal York Hotel in which Victoria and her mother stayed is No. 24, and still retains some of the original furniture. A plaque over the door proclaims that 'Her Majesty the Queen, when Princess Victoria, accompanied by her mother, the Duchess of Kent, occupied this room, October, 1830'.

During their visit, the Princess and her mother purchased jewellery from the shop of Payne & Sons—now Mallory's—on Old Bond Street. The splendid royal coat-of-arms adorning the parapet of the shop, and facing Milsom Street, dates from this time.

WADE, Field-Marshal George (1673-1748)
*14 Abbey Churchyard

Field-Marshal Wade, whose house stands in Abbey Churchyard, was one of Bath's most celebrated residents during the first half of the eighteenth century. He had

105

served with distinction under Marlborough in Belgium, and was promoted general at the age of 35. Soon afterwards, he was sent to Bath to quell Jacobite plots and uprisings that occurred frequently in the area between 1715 and 1720. In 1725, as Commander-in-Chief, Scotland, his reputation was further enhanced by the fine military roads he built there.

But Wade always spent part of each year in Bath. He commenced building his house in Abbey Churchyard round about 1720, and he served four times as MP for the city between 1722 and 1748. His natural daughter, Miss Earl, married Ralph Allen, and it was Wade's influence and financial support that enabled Allen to become Bath's postmaster.

Field-Marshal Wade died in 1748, and was buried in Westminster Abbey. The house in Abbey Churchyard, with its impressive façade dominated by five Ionic pilasters, is described by Walter Ison in his *Georgian Buildings of Bath* as 'probably the earliest example in Bath of the Palladian use of a giant order'. It is now occupied by the National Trust, and the bronze tablet that adorns the façade was unveiled by Field-Marshal Lord Methuen in October, 1924.

WALPOLE, Horace (1717-1797)
Chapel Court

Of the many prodigious letter-writers of the eighteenth century, Horace Walpole was arguably the most brilliant and entertaining. He wrote something like 3,000 letters, a great many of them witty, epigrammatic and vastly interesting. He turned a modest house in Twickenham into a mock Gothic castle, and called it Strawberry Hill; and there, with generous funds provided by his father, he lived the life of a dilettante, writing and enjoying his substantial collection of books, pictures and curios.

He came to Bath in 1766, and stayed at a house in Chapel Court for three months. 'Walpole passed many a day there', wrote Thackeray, 'sickly, supercilious, absurdly dandified and affected; with a brilliant wit, a delightful sensibility; and, for his friends, a most tender, generous and faithful heart'. But Horace didn't like Bath. The local hills annoyed him: 'One cannot stir out of the town without clambering', he wrote to a friend. And he disliked the new buildings: 'They look like a collection of little hospitals—all crammed together, and surrounded with perpendicular hills. Oh! how unlike my lovely Thames!' His ultimate judgment on the city was equally disparaging: 'These watering places that mimic a capital, and add vulgarisms and familiarities of their own, seem to me like Abigail in cast gowns, and I am not young enough to take up with either'. Like Jane Austen later, he left Bath with undisguised feelings of relief.

WEATHERLEY, Fred (1848-1929)
10 Edward Street

Fred Weatherley was an accomplished lyricist, who wrote the words for many well-known songs, including *Danny Boy, Roses of Picardy* and *Friend o' Mine*. Like his famous near-contemporary W.S. Gilbert (the lyricist of the Savoy operas), he was called to the Bar; but legal work never prevented him from writing songs, and he published more than 1,500 in his long lifetime. He lived at No. 10 Edward Street from 1919 until 1928, and there is a bronze tablet on the house proclaiming his occupancy. He died at Bathwick Lodge, Bathwick Hill, in September, 1929.

WEDGWOOD, Josiah (1730-1795)
Westgate Buildings; 30 Gay Street

The celebrated potter came to Bath in the summer of 1772, and opened a showroom in Westgate Buildings, where his distinctive wares were attractively displayed. Mrs. Wedgwood accompanied him, hoping that a course of Bath waters would assuage her rheumatism. Wedgwood wrote to a friend: 'The season seems completely over here, and the town is scarcely habitable for heat. We take a mouthful of fresh air on the Downs in the morning, drink three or four glasses of scalding hot water from the Pump, and sweat it out in the least hot places we find out the remainder of the day'. Unhappily, Mrs. Wedgwood's affliction was not improved by the treatment, and they returned to Staffordshire. Wedgwood came back to the city more than twenty years later, and is said to have lodged at No. 30 Gay Street.

WESLEY, John (1703-1791)
2 Broad Street

The founder of Methodism preached in London for the first time in 1738, and visited Bath in the following year. His first two sermons in the city attracted five thousand people, and he was heard to exclaim: 'Can the Gospel have a place where Satan's throne is?'. Beau Nash, probably resenting the implication that he was the Devil personified, indulged in a heated exchange of words with the evangelist, and is said to have lost the debate.

Wesley was later described by Horace Walpole as 'a lean, elderly man, fresh-coloured, his hair smoothly combed, but
108

with a *soupçon* of curl at the ends. Wondrous clean, but as evidently an actor as Garrick'. He came to Bath several times, and usually lodged at No. 2 Broad Street. In 1777 he laid the foundation stone of the original Methodist chapel in the city, in New King Street, and opened the building two years later. It was replaced by a second chapel that was destroyed in an air-raid in 1942; and a plaque on the site, placed there in 1979, commemorates the 200th anniversary of the original opening.

WHISTLER, James Abbot McNeill (1834-1903)
7 Marlborough Street

The controversial American painter of the late nineteenth century lived abroad during most of his life, chiefly in France and England. In England he was closely associated with the school of thought that wished to divorce art from social, literary or anecdotal significance; the famous portrait of his mother, for example, is prosaically entitled *Arrangement in Grey and Black.* He was greatly interested in Japanese prints, and from this source he adapted the butterfly symbol that he used to sign his later paintings.

He setted in Tite Street, Chelsea, in 1880; and during the last two years of his life, he lived for a time at No. 7 Marlborough Street, in Bath. His influence on contemporary art has been immense.

WILBERFORCE, William (1759-1833)
*36 Great Pulteney Street

'He was an agitator who always retained his powerful gift

of social charm, the outcome of his sweet disposition'. Thus wrote Trevelyan about the man who is always remembered for his leadership of the campaign to abolish the slave trade and slavery. He lived at No. 9 North Parade in 1831, and at No. 36 Great Pulteney Street in 1802 and 1805, where there is a bronze tablet recording his stay there. He married Barbara Spooner at Walcot Church in 1797; her parents had a house at No. 2 Royal Crescent, and he was a frequent visitor there, spending a winter holiday during the parliamentary recess late in 1798. His bill for the abolition of slavery had just been defeated for the fourth time; it was finally carried in the House of Commons in 1804, and after twice being rejected by the Lords, it was given the royal assent in 1807.

Wilberforce, according to a contemporary who frequently encountered him in the Octagon Chapel in Bath, was 'a small, delicate looking man with an intelligent eye, and his head reclining to one side'. He was an altruist; to quote Trevelyan again: 'With his talents and position, he would probably have been Pitt's successor as Prime Minister, if he had preferred party to mankind. His sacrifice of one kind of fame and power, gave him another and a nobler title to remembrance'.

WILCOX, Ella Wheeler (1850-1919)
9 Upper Church Street

The first book of poems that Ella Wheeler Wilcox produced had the unpromising title *Drops of Water;* it was a collection of temperance verses. She next wrote *Poems of Passion,* which was immediately rejected by a publisher, creating a mild sensation and engendering much useful publicity. A second publisher enterprisingly produced the
110

book, and it proved to be a great success. Thereafter, Mrs. Wilcox wrote extensively, and her poems were much in demand by journals and magazines. Her work was widely criticised on the grounds that it was platitudinous and over-sentimental; but she always defended herself by claiming that her poetry gave a great deal of comfort to many weary and unhappy people—which it probably did.

During 1918 she toured army camps in France, reciting her poems and delivering talks on sexual problems. She became ill through over-exertion and came to Bath, where she spent some months in the spring of 1919 in a nursing home at No. 9 Upper Church Street, before returning to the United States. She died three months after her homecoming.

WILKES, John (1727-1797)
12 South Parade; 5 Galloway's Buildings (now North Parade Buildings)

John Wilkes can be mildly described as a massive thorn in the flesh of the reactionary eighteenth-century establishment. He was arrested for libelling George III, and was twice expelled from the House of Commons, and imprisoned, for his outspoken views. He was elected MP for Middlesex several times, and was Lord Mayor of London in 1774. He worked unceasingly for the liberty of the individual and freedom of the press. He called himself 'a patriot by accident', and 'a friend of liberty'; and he was reviled by almost everyone in the corridors of power.

He came to Bath several times between 1772 and 1778, and lodged at No. 12 South Parade and No. 5 Galloway's Buildings (now North Parade Buildings). Ostensibly, he came for the waters; but he loved the city for its gay society, and his sharp wit always found a ready outlet there. His diary is often amusing; for example, he wrote of his landlady at Galloway's Buildings: 'Miss Temple has just dropped me such a broad wheel courtesy that I trembled for the floor, and the floor trembled likewise'. And the love he cherished for his only daughter, Polly, is evident from this note that he wrote to her from Bath on Christmas day, 1778: 'Polly, dear sweet Polly, I have a new coat and it is all blue, and it has a fine edging, and I have a fine silk waistcoat . . . and fine mother-of-pearl buttons, in every one of which you might see your pretty face. I am undoubtedly the greatest fop in Bath'.

For many years a small, dingy obelisk, dedicated to 'the Right Honourable John Wilkes Esq, Lord Mayor of London', stood in Ludgate Circus, above the entrance to a subterranean gentleman's lavatory. Many of his political opponents would have happily considered it to be most appropriately sited.

WOLFE, James, General (1727-1759)
5 Trim Street

In 1759, when he was only thirty-two, Wolfe, was appointed to command the force that was sent to take Quebec, and thereby open Canada to British conquest. His troops, after scaling the Heights of Abraham by night, surprised and defeated the French under Montcalm, and Quebec was captured. In the closing stages of the battle, Wolfe was mortally wounded by a musket ball and carried behind the lines; and when news of the victory was brought to him he uttered, with his last breath, the famous words 'Now God be praised, I will die in peace'.

He had often visited Bath, staying with his parents who

Mrs. Thrale—portrait by unknown Italian artist.

George Wade—portrait attributed to Johann van Diest.

Horace Walpole—portrait by J. G. Eccardt.

James Wolfe—portrait attributed to J. S. C. Schaak.

had taken a house at No. 5 Trim Street. After returning to England following the siege of Louisbourg in 1758, he wrote to a friend from Salisbury: 'My health is mightily impaired by the long confinement at sea. I am going to Bath to refit for another campaign'. Shortly afterwards, he was given command of the Quebec expedition.

On the day before he embarked for Canada, he was invited to dine with the elder Pitt at No. 7 the Circus. During the visit he antagonised his host by drawing his sword, boasting of his prowess as a soldier, and aggressively describing what he intended to do when he reached Quebec; and after he had left, Pitt voiced his regret to another guest 'at confiding the fate of the administration, and of the country, to so vain-glorious a boaster'.

Wolfe may have been conceited, but he was undoubtedly brave and resourceful. He was something of a romantic, too: during the ascent of the Heights of Abraham, he was heard reciting stanzas from Gray's *Elegy Written in a Country Churchyard*, and asserting that he would rather have been the author of that poem than take Quebec. And after his death, it was discovered that he was wearing a miniature portrait of a young woman next to his heart. She was a Miss Lowther of Bath, a close friend whom he had known and admired for some time.

WOOD, John, the Elder (1704-1754)
24 Queen Square

The elder Wood has been described as 'the pioneer who brought Bath from being an insignificant little town into the mainstream of European architecture'. He was born in the city, but much of his early career was spent in Yorkshire and London; he returned to Bath in 1727, and there his

113

architectural genius found its fullest expression.

He was a confirmed disciple of the Palladian school, a style named after the sixteenth-century Italian architect, Andrea Palladio, and his ambitious plan was to make Bath the Rome of Britain, with a Forum, a Circus Maximus and other comparable buildings. The Corporation received his scheme with a marked lack of enthusiasm; but he was an entrepreneur and a business man as well as an architect, and the need to satisfy the growing demand for accommodation in the city soon began to occupy most of his time. Work on Queen Square, named in honour of George II's consort, Caroline, was commenced in 1729, and continued for seven years. The northern terrace of the square is particularly fine: Bryan Little has described it as 'Bath's most important piece of architecture . . . a set of lodgings becomes a palace'. Wood took one of the centre houses—No. 24—for himself.

Later, he built Prior Park, Ralph Allen's splendid mansion on the outskirts of the city. But his greatest achievement was the Circus, which was commenced in 1754. Wood died only three months after laying the foundation stone of the first house; but the work was completed by his son, John Wood, also an outstanding architect, in 1769.

Wood died at his house in Queen Square in 1754, and a bronze tablet commemorates his occupancy. He was buried in the chancel of Swainswick Church.

WOOD, John the Younger (1728-1801)
41 Gay Street

The achievement of the younger John Wood is considered by some authorities to surpass even that of his father. After completing the Circus following the elder Wood's death, he built the incomparable Royal Crescent between 1767 and

1775, linking it to the Circus with Brock Street, which he named after his brother-in-law; and almost simultaneously, his designs for the new Assembly Rooms saw fruition. Alfred Street and Bennett Street were also his creations.

He was trained assiduously by his father, and when the elder Wood went to Liverpool to build a new town hall, his son accompanied him. It was there he met his future wife, who was the sister of Chester's town clerk, Thomas Brock. The couple were married in 1752, and settled in Bath at No. 41 Gay Street, an attractive house that had been designed by the elder Wood, with an elaborate corner bow facing Queen Square. Here they brought up a family of seven girls and two boys.

Towards the end of his life he was deeply concerned over the poor housing conditions of labourers and artisans. The overcrowding, and the damp, unhealthy nature of most of the ramshackle, unsanitary cottages in which they lived, appalled him; and in 1780 he published *A Series of Plans for Cottages and Habitations of the Labourer, either in Husbandry or the Mechanic's Arts,* in which he undoubtedly staked a claim to be the first social reformer in architecture. He died in 1801, and was buried beside his father in the chancel of Swainswick Church.

WORDSWORTH, William (1770-1850)
9 North Parade

Two years before he succeeded Southey as Poet Laureate, Wordsworth visited Bath, and on 29th April, 1841, the *Chronicle* briefly announced his presence in the city: 'The distinguished poet Wordsworth is at present residing in Bath, where we understand he will remain until the middle of June'.

There is a bronze tablet on the wall of No. 9 North Parade, commemorating the poet's visit. It is, it seems, misplaced; at the head of a letter he wrote to a friend during his stay, his address is clearly stated as No. 12 North Parade—which leaves little doubt about the identity of the house. Wordsworth visited Walter Savage Landor at No. 35 St. James's Square while he was in Bath; and towards the end of his visit he attended the wedding of his only daughter, Dora, to Mr. Edward Quillinan at St. James's Church. This church was gutted by fire in 1942, during the 'Baedeker' air raids on Bath, and was subsequently demolished to make room for the erection of Woolworth's store in Stall Street.

Key to map

Because of space restrictions, the house positions on the map are approximate.

THEY CAME TO BATH
A street-by-street guide

Abbey Church House
Queen Anne

Abbey Church Yard
No. 5—Percy Bysshe Shelley
No. 14—Field-Marshal George Wade

Alfred Street
No. 2—Sir Thomas Lawrence
       Mrs. Catharine Macaulay

Argyle Street
Chapel—Rev. William Jay
No. 8—John Jervis, Earl St. Vincent

Bathwick Street
No. 16—Benjamin Barker

Belvedere
No. 8—Edward Gibbon

Bennett Street
No. 19—Vice-Admiral Arthur Phillip

Broad Street
No. 2—John Wesley

Brock Street
No. 8—Benjamin Disraeli, 1st Earl of Beaconsfield
No. 18—John Christopher Smith

Catharine Place
No. 12—Admiral Sir Sydney Smith

Cavendish Road
Doric House—Thomas Barker

Chapel Court
Horace Walpole

Charles Street

No. 22—Edward Gibbon

Circus, the

No. 7—William Pitt, the Elder, Lord Chatham
No. 9—Lord Frederic Leighton
No. 13—David Livingstone
No. 14—Lord Robert Clive
No. 17—Thomas Gainsborough
　　　　　William Makepeace Thackeray
No. 22—Major John André
No. 27—Dr. Caleb Hillier Parry
　　　　　Sir William Edward Parry
No. 29—Dr. William Falconer

The Corridor

No. 9—William Friese-Green

Edward Street

No. 6—Lady Emma Hamilton
No. 10—Fred Weatherley

Galloway's Buildings (Now North Parade Buildings)

No. 5—John Wilkes

Gay Street

No. 2—Admiral Sir Edward Berry
No. 8—Mrs. Hester Thrale
No. 13—Venanzio Rauzzini
No. 23—William Friese-Green
No. 30—Josiah Wedgwood
No. 41—John Wood, the Elder
　　　　　Tobias Smollett

George Street

No. 4 Edgar Buildings—Selina, Countess of Huntingdon
No. 5 Princes Buildings—Prince Hoare
No. 6 Edgar Buildings—William Hoare
No. 13—Henry Stafford Smith
Royal York Hotel—Queen Victoria

122

Great Pulteney Street

No. 2—Lord Edward Bulwer-Lytton, 1st Baron Lytton

No. 27—Maria Anne Fitzherbert

No. 29—William Smith

No. 34—Admiral Alexander Hood, Viscount Bridport

No. 36—William Wilberforce

No. 53—Marie Dolores Eliza Gilbert, Countess of
Lansfeldt known as Lola Montez

No. 55—Louis Napoleon Bonaparte, Napoleon III

No. 59—Connop Thirlwall, Bishop of St. David's

No. 71—Admiral William Howe, Earl Howe

No. 72—King Louis XVIII of France

No. 76—Hannah More

Pulteney Hotel—Prince Arthur, Duke of Connaught

Green Park

No. 6—Thomas de Quincey

No. 19—Sir William Francis Patrick Napier

Henrietta Street

No. 8—Moses Pickwick

No. 10—Sir Charles James Napier

Johnstone Street

No. 15—William Pitt, the Younger

Lansdown Crescent

No. 19—William Beckford

No. 20—William Beckford

Lansdown Grove Hotel—Yehudi Menuhin

Laura Place

No. 7—Moses Pickwick

Lilliput Alley

between York Street and North Parade Passage—Ralph
Allen

Lyncombe
Perrymead Villa—Franz Joseph Haydn
Venanzio Rauzzini

Lymore Gardens
Albert Semprini

Marlborough Buildings
No. 9—Jan Morris
No. 22—Lady Betty Cobbe

Marlborough Street
No. 7—James Abbot McNeill Whistler

New King Street
No. 9—Richard Brinsley Sheridan
No. 19—Sir William Herschel

Norfolk Buildings
No. 8—Sir Bartle Frere

North Parade
No. 9—William Wordsworth
No. 11—Edmund Burke
Oliver Goldsmith
David Garrick

North Parade Buildings
No. 1—John Palmer

North Parade Passage
Sally Lunn

Orange Grove
Henrietta Knight, Lady Luxborough

Paragon, the
No. 33—Sarah Siddons

Park Street
No. 34—Admiral Volant Vashon Ballard

124

Pierrepont Place
Elizabeth Linley

Pierrepont Street
No. 2—Horatio Nelson, 1st Viscount Nelson
No. 3—James Quin
          George Frederic Handel
No. 3A—Philip Dormer Stanhope, 4th Earl of Chesterfield
No. 4—Philip Dormer Stanhope, 4th Earl of Chesterfield

Portland Place
No. 17—Thomas Robert Malthus

Prior Park
Alexander Pope
Ralph Allen

Queen Square
No. 17—Venanzio Rauzzini
No. 24—John Wood, the Elder
West Side—William Oliver M.D.
Francis Hotel—Lord Peter Thorneycroft

Queen's Parade
No. 9—Field-Marshal Lord Frederick Roberts (Earl)

Rivers Street
No. 3—Walter Savage Landor

Royal Crescent
No. 1—Princess Marie Thérèse de Lamballe
          Frederick Augustus, Duke of York
No. 1A—George Saintsbury
No. 5—Christopher Anstey
No. 8—Vicomte Jean Baptiste du Barré
No. 9—Admiral Sir William Hargood
          Lord Edward Bulwer-Lytton, 1st Baron Lytton
          Philip Thicknesse

No. 10—Frederic Harrison
No. 11—Elizabeth Linley
No. 15—Dr. John Haygarth
No. 16—Frederick Augustus, Duke of York
   Mrs. Elizabeth Montagu
   Sir Francis Burdett
   Baroness Angela Georgina Burdett-Coutts
No. 17—Mary, Countess of Belmore
   Sir Isaac Pitman
No. 20—Fanny Sage
No. 22—Lady Celia Noble
Royal Crescent Hotel—Lord Laurence Olivier
     Sir Ralph Richardson

Sawclose
'Beau' Nash

South Parade
No. 5—Elizabeth Chudleigh, Duchess of Kingston
No. 6—Sir Walter Scott
No. 7—Tobias Smollett
No. 12—John Wilkes
   John Hunter
No. 14—Fanny Burney

Sydney Place
No. 4—Jane Austen
No. 93—Queen Charlotte
No. 103—Duke of Clarence

St. George's Hill (Bathampton)
Walter Richard Sickert

St. James' Square
No. 35—Walter Savage Landor
   Charles Dickens

St. John's Court
'Beau' Nash
126

Trim Street
No. 5—General James Wolfe

Twerton
Fielding's Lodge—Henry Fielding

Upper Church Street
No. 9—Ella Wheeler Wilcox

Walcot Street
No. 108—Robert Southey
Pelican Inn—Samuel Johnson

Westgate Buildings
Josiah Wedgwood

Widcombe Lodge
Henry Fielding
Sarah Fielding

Widcombe Crescent
No. 1—Sir James Brooke